WEAVE US TOGETHER

My Musical Journey

Rosemary Crow

Cover design by Leslie Flanagan
Interior design by Diana Wade

Printed in the United States of America

Published by Old Crow Press

Contents

for Jerry,
always the first listener of my songs,
who encouraged me every step of the way.

Rosemary Crow's music is not superficial and integrates all of our fragmented selves so that the body, mind, and spirit sing forth with one joyful voice.

—Madeleine L'Engle, Author

ುಲ

A bit of Rosemary is enough to last you three or four lifetimes. A word from Rosemary is similar, only better. You read this and you'll feel invigorated, refreshed, and transformed. To read Rosemary is to fall in love with life.

The Rev. Howard Hanger, Methodist Minister, Musician, and Founder of Jubilee! Community in Asheville, NC

WEAVE

We are many textures, we are many colors,
Each on diff'rent from the other.
But we are entwined with one another
In one great tapestry.

REFRAIN
Weave, weave, weave us together.
Weave us together in unity and love.
Weave, weave, weave us together.
Weave us together, together in love.

We are diff'rent instruments playing our own melodies,
Each one tuning to a diff'rent key.
But we are all playing in harmony
In one great symphony.

REFRAIN
A moment ago, still we did not know
Our unity, only diversity.
Now the Christ in me greet the Christ in thee
In one great family.

REFRAIN

Listen to the music deep within you.
God is there.

Acknowledgments

Thanks to Dershie for giving me a crash course in writing and to Linda for her careful reading and editing.

Thanks to my editor, Betsy, for her skill, patience and humor and to my formatter, Diana, for her careful attention to detail and thanks to my daughter, Leslie for the cover design.

Thanks to my first readers, Sharon, Martha, Carter, and Sam for their generous gift of time and helpful comments.

Thanks to my prayer group, Mary Beth, Harriet, Lucy, Mary, Randy and Jeanette who listened to my first song.

Thanks to the Whales and the Wise Women, Susan, Julie, Jeanne, Mimi, Charlotte, and Gwenda who encouraged me.

Thanks to the clergy who praised my music, Bud, Grahame, Harry, and Bishop Weinhauer.

Special thanks to my three friends, Howard, Mary Beth, and Mimi who made my journey easier with their incredible talents.

Thanks to my children, Sam and Leslie and my husband Jerry, who waved goodby with a smile and welcomed me home with open arms after my music travels.

Finally, thanks to each of you who listened to and sang my music.

Prologue

I have always been a singer. At the age of ten, I was singing solos in school and at church. I had a big voice for such a young person, and most of the time I enjoyed being a singer. But sometimes it was a burden. Like the times when my parents had guests for dinner and after they arrived, my dad would ask them, "Have you heard Rosemary sing"? Most of the time they already had several times, but someone would graciously say, "No. We'd like to hear her." I would be sitting at the top of the stairs waiting, knowing that I would hear Dad's voice from downstairs calling me, "Rosemary, would you please come down and sing for our guests?"

Music was in my blood; my parents gave me the chance to develop my talent. I took piano lessons through elementary and junior high school, and began voice lessons when I was in high school. I earned a Bachelor of Music degree at Salem College in Winston-Salem, North Carolina. During college, I met Jerry who had come to my hometown, Coral Gables, Florida to be in a wedding. The next fall, he called me at college to say that he would be in Salisbury for Thanksgiving and would like to come see me. I was not going to be there over the holidays so we made a date for early December. He was living in Asheville, which was only three hours away. After our first date, we began seeing each other every other weekend and soon fell in love. The following year, he entered Wake Forest Law School, conveniently located just across town from Salem. We were engaged my senior year with plans to marry that summer after I graduated. I changed my major from Vocal Performance to Public School Music, because I knew that I would need to find work while he completed his last two years of law school. I taught in the Winston-Salem Public Schools, traveling between three schools teaching music in an elementary school, and chorus in a junior high and a high school. I was an idealistic first-year teacher. I had loved the musical "The King and I," so just like Anna in the play, I sang "Getting to Know You" to my students in my first class of junior high chorus. Those young teenagers' jaws dropped and their eyes widened like they thought I was crazy. I was embarrassed and decided that I would never do that again.

After Jerry graduated from law school, he was commissioned as a First Lieutenant in the Army's Judge Advocates' Corps. We were thrilled that his orders sent us to Fort Ord in Monterey, California, because it would be an adventure to live in a state so far from home. Once again that Public School Music degree came in handy; I got a position teaching in a brand-new high school which meant there was no more traveling from school to school. Our son, Sam was born the last year that we were there, so I stopped teaching to be a full-time mom.

When Jerry's army tour was over, he took a job in his hometown, Asheville, North Carolina. Soon after our arrival, our daughter Leslie was born. I was an even busier full-time mom, but missed music, which had always been simmering on my back burner. One day I learned that a small neighborhood Presbyterian church was looking for a choir director. I talked it over with Jerry and since my job responsibilities would only be one night a week for choir practices and for Sunday morning services, I would still have plenty of time at home with the children. I took the job and enjoyed directing adults. However, I did miss the Episcopal Church. I had been raised in the Methodist Church, but attended St Paul's Episcopal Church in Winston-Salem while in college. I loved the liturgy and the music, so I joined the choir and soon after was confirmed during my senior year at Salem.

A couple of years later, I heard through the grapevine that Trinity Episcopal Church downtown was looking for a Director of Music. The rector was away on sabbatical, so I made an appointment and talked with the young priest in charge. He talked with the rector who said that he had doubts about hiring me, because in the past there had been only one person who would simultaneously play the organ and direct the choirs. Now he wondered that if he hired two people, could they get along with each other? I interviewed with the rector on the phone, and with the young priest's support, I got the job. He also interviewed a young man to be the organist and he was hired.

I felt a little inadequate because I had not had any formal training in church music with chanting psalms and canticles, nor in planning the Sunday liturgy. Before my first week on the job, I called the Music Director at the other large Episcopal church in town and asked if he could give me a crash course. He went over the Hymnal in great detail, especially the service music. He taught me how to sing the canticles for Morning Prayer and the service music for Communion. He explained how he planned the music to enhance the appointed lssons and Gospel readings for each Sunday. After an afternoon with him, I felt that I could wing it. And so I did.

I was really an ordinary and happy wife, mother, and church choir director, when I was catapulted into a world of composing, singing, recording, and traveling that I could never have imagined. This is where my memoir begins.......

Holy Silence

I hear Thy voice in the wind and rain,
The stillness of the stars by night.
In the ocean's roar is Thy name again.
Thy still, small voice is my delight.

I heard her singing just as I was falling asleep. It was May 14, 1976, my 38th birthday. Irritated that I had a bad cold and was feeling lousy, I had laid down to take a nap. Just as I was drifting off, I heard a woman's voice singing in my head. She had a mezzo-soprano voice just like mine and sang, "Speak to me in holy silence." Her singing was crystal clear, but I was already in the state between being awake and falling asleep, so I drifted off. When I awoke, I tried to remember what had happened. I had heard a woman's voice, but hadn't seen her and couldn't remember the melody that she'd sung. *Was it only a dream? Would I ever hear it again?* I went to the piano and began noodling around, playing random notes and chords.

To my amazement, the entire song emerged, complete with words and music. I couldn't believe it. I had never even thought of composing a song. *What was happening? Where did that voice come from and would I ever hear it again?* I stayed at the piano playing the music over and over; then I found some blank paper and drew out a staff and wrote down the notes so that I wouldn't forget it. It was truly a brand-new song. What a birthday gift!

The genesis of the song must have come from my daily meditations. Six years ago, I'd been invited by my friend, Harriet, to join her small prayer group which met every Wednesday morning and these women had become dear friends. We journaled, paid attention to our dreams which we wrote down to share with each other, and tried to meditate daily. All of these experiences had been calling me into a deep and vivid inner life. Our prayer group had a weekly discipline to meditate on a phrase, and the week that the song had come to me, the phrase had been "holy silence." I couldn't wait to tell them about my experience.

When Wednesday finally arrived, I was bursting inside with my news, but waited for just the right time to tell them. As usual, we greeted and hugged one another, got our coffee, and then sat in a circle for our meeting. Each one of us was to report on our response to the phrase that we had meditated on. I sat quietly, but churning inside waiting for my turn. When it finally came, I excitedly told them what had happened to me and that I'd composed the song, "Holy Silence." Mary, our host, had an old out-of-tune upright piano in the basement, and I asked if I could go downstairs and play my song. As the eight women stood at the top of the stairs, I sang and played.

They were stunned by my offering and after I finished, I ran up the stairs and we began to all talk at once. There was much laughter, and Mary had tears of joy. We each sensed that something important and wonderful had happened. One woman said, "You have been given a deep, spiritual gift. You are being used as a channel to bring new songs into being." I was overwhelmed by their response.

I wondered if I would ever hear another one?

In the next week, I was compelled to sit at the piano and noodle again, waiting and hoping to hear another song. I had sometimes played around on the piano in the past with different chords and melodies, but this time it was different; I sat expectantly waiting to hear another song. To my great joy and surprise, two more songs came pouring in. "God the Father" was a snappy, almost rock song, and another simple song came "Know the Truth." After that, I couldn't stay away from noodling at the piano, just waiting and listening.

My seat at the piano offered me a view through expansive glass doors of two acres of dense forest with majestic maple and oak trees on our property. But one tree drew my attention. It was a scrawny black walnut on the edge of the woods closest to me. Its leaves were alive and shimmering in the sunlight as if it were sending me the vibrations of the music. Could it be? Was the tree helping me hear the music? Yes. I felt that the dancing leaves were awakening my heart and ears to listen for this new inner music. Later, when I showed my special tree to Jerry, he said, "You mean that scraggly walnut tree?" I laughed and said, "Yes. That's the one!" The songs kept coming and it was like a dam of music had burst inside of me. I couldn't stay away from my piano, nor from looking at that tree!

A whirlwind of creativity filled my next two weeks, and I composed eight songs. I wanted to understand what was happening to me, so I began reading about musicians, artists, poets, and writers, and their creative processes. Some had amazing stories. Madeline L'Engle's book *Walking on Water* resonated with me when she described her writing process. She talked about the two Greek words for time: "chronos" which is everyday time and "kairos" which is time in another dimension. She wrote, "When my writing is flowing, it is like turning a key and walking through the door into kairos where there is no time and no space. I couldn't make it happen, but I knew when I was in that place." My experience was the same. It happened most frequently when I was at the piano, noodling. I couldn't make a song come, but like L'Engle, I knew when the key turned and I passed through that door into sacred space. Then the music and words came flowing in. Time stood still and I could sit at the piano for hours, even though it would seem as if only a few minutes had passed. Sometimes it was just a melody and the words came later. Then I would work with matching the words to the melody and rhythm. Sometimes I would have words running around in my head for days, and then during my noodling the melody would come.

I did think about asking God, "Why are you only sending me simple songs? How about a cantata, or at least a four-part anthem?" Then I imagined God smiling as He said, "That's all you can handle, dear." I remembered what a music snob I'd been until I'd recently gone to a conference at St. Luke's Episcopal Church in Atlanta on "New Music for Worship." Peter Yarrow of "Peter, Paul, and Mary" was one of the leaders. He was a small, balding man full of joy and energy and reminded me of an elf as he seemed to dance when he led us in singing the old song, "Rocka my soul." He truly held us in the palms of his hands as he signaled us to sing loud or soft, and then fast or slow. It was a moving experience to sing with those hundred people as if we were one voice. Peter told us a fable about a singer who discovered that the secret of solo singing was not the singer nor the song, but the people's singing the song that mattered most of all. That was an "aha" moment for me; I realized what a gift God had given me with my simple songs that all kinds of people could sing.

When I returned from Atlanta, at our Wednesday Prayer Group, I found out that some of our members had gone to hear Jim Goure speak at the University of North Carolina at Asheville. Jim was a retired United States Navy nuclear physicist who had come to Black Mountain to build a geodesic dome which he called a Light Center. He said that his mission was to pray for the planet and to teach others to pray 24/7, so that there would always be someone praying in the Light Center. The next Wednesday, the group decided to go out to Black Mountain to meet him, rather than go to our regular meeting. As I drove in, he began walking towards my car and as I got out, he approached me and said, "I have been waiting for you."

"No," I said, "I've never met you before."

He looked deeply into my eyes and it was as if he was looking into my soul and had always known me. I had an inner sense that he was going to be an important part of my life. Jim was a tall man who cut an imposing figure with his erect Navy posture. His eyes were deep blue, magical and mysterious. He invited us inside and we sat around his spacious living room that was filled with light from the large windows overlooking the mountains. We were intrigued when he offered to teach us to pray in four lessons on four successive Fridays. That was the beginning of the Friday group, which lasted way beyond the four weeks and continued meeting for many years. Jim was a psychic/mystic and unlike anyone I had ever met. *Was he crazy, brilliant, delusional or all three?* Every Friday, he taught a class with mind-blowing ideas about religion, prayer, and the unseen world. He talked of communicating with great Beings in the spirit world. He said, "They told me that our planet was in need of unceasing prayer and my mission is to teach others to pray." His lectures and thoughts were the inspiration for many of my songs.

As the weeks went by, I wrote more and more songs. I began singing them for our Wednesday prayer group and for Jim's Friday group. Years before I had given up my solo singing and instead settled for teaching and directing the choir at Trinity. But now, I *needed* to sing, since I was the only one who knew these new songs. Surprisingly, my voice was still true and clear, and I began to realize how much I had missed singing for people. It was like getting on my childhood bicycle that I rode long ago and discovering that I could still ride.

The folks in both groups liked the songs and wanted me to record them. I thought that was crazy. I had no clue how to make a recording, but knew that if I did, I would want to go to a recording studio where the sound would be pure and undistorted. I screwed up my courage and called my friend, jazz pianist, Howard Hanger. He was a successful musician as well as an ordained Methodist minister. He had composed and recorded several record albums and traveled to many places in our country and overseas with his Howard Hanger Trio. He answered the phone and I excitedly told him, "Howard, I'm writing songs. Do I need to copyright them?"

He chuckled and calmly said, "Don't worry. There's no rush. I don't think anyone will try to steal them."

I asked, "Could you and your jazz trio help me record an album?"

He hesitantly said, "Possibly."

"Do you know of a good local studio?"

"A friend of mine has a small home-made 4 track studio."

"What do you think it would cost?"

"Probably cost around $2,000 to pay for studio time, the musicians, and the cost of producing records and cassette tapes."

I was flabbergasted. "There's no way I could fork out $2,000!" That was a huge amount of money in 1976, and several times more than my monthly salary at Trinity. I thanked him and hung up the phone.

Maybe the songs were not even good enough to record. Probably only a few people would buy the records and then I would be out all that money. My logical side was fast talking me out of the whole project.

Then an amazing thing happened. Out of the blue, Brigitte, a member of Jim's Friday group, called me to ask if she could come over. I was surprised that she wanted to come over as she was only an acquaintance. When she asked about my recording an album, I said, "I've looked into it and it's cost-prohibitive; around $2,000."

"I will give you the $2,000," she said.

I was stunned. How could I accept so large a gift? Was this a sign from God that the songs were worthy of recording and that people would want to hear them? I talked it over with Jerry, and we decided that I would ask Brigitte for an interest-free loan. She agreed. Jerry was supportive of my music and this new venture, and Howard said that he was sure I could recoup my investment. So I accepted her $2,000 check, wondering how I would ever repay her.

Finally I was committed to proceed, and called Howard. He suggested that we get together to work on the musical arrangements. We agreed to meet at his house, which was a huge, partially restored

Victorian mansion in a neighborhood called Chicken Hill. It was in an area with run-down houses, rusty old cars, and an abandoned bus depot across the street. My palms were sweating as I went up on the large porch, approached the enormous front door, and banged the door knocker. No one answered. I banged again louder and still no one appeared. I tried the doorknob and it was unlocked. My heart cranked up about twenty beats. I stepped inside and my voice cracked as I timidly called "Howard." Still no one came, so I called out louder, "Howard!" After what seemed like a long, long time, he came out from one of the rooms and walked down the creaky wooden hall. Howard was a recovering hippie, and his many renters were an eclectic rag-tag bunch of artists. "Dear God," I prayed, "did you really lead me here—a buttoned-down, ill-at-ease church musician?" I was in over my head in this strange environment and felt crazy to be spending $2,000 that wasn't even mine!

Howard escorted me into his room and sat down at his baby grand piano. I timidly pulled out my folder, afraid that he would think my simple songs were not up to his standards. There were twenty-eight songs, and he said, "First, you need to decide on ten or twelve that you want to record." I selected "Be Still," because that was the one that most people requested when I was singing. Another, "All He Has is Thee" made the list. It combined an ancient plainsong chant of "Magnificat" with my song which said, "He must be Born in Thee." Others were "Jericho," "Peace," and seven more, which totaled eleven songs.

After I'd made my selections, Howard began reading my music sheets and played "Be Still." His rendition was beautiful. I instantly relaxed and knew that all would be well. While he played through all the songs, I was transported as he made the harmonies sound rich and complex. We began to decide which instruments each song needed for texture and color. He used my original chords in his arrangements, but enriched them with extra notes and rhythms. He suggested some good, local instrumentalists and told me how to contact them and how much to offer to pay them.

Howard was a man full of energy and enthusiasm, who made me feel that he was glad to work with me and that my songs were worthy of his efforts. That was the beginning of a joyous musical relationship with this creative and talented man.

When we were finally ready to record, we contracted with Howard's friend for his studio and his expertise in sound engineering. I'd already contacted Eli, the bass player, Beth the violinist and singer, and A.D., the guitarist, who each agreed to play on the album. Then we made a date for Howard and the instrumentalists to meet with me at the studio one night. Howard said, "It has to be at night, because that's when musicians are the most creative." Night was anything but conducive to *my* creativity, because we had two children who got me up early and kept me busy: Sam, who was eleven and Leslie, who was nine. I was worn out by nightfall, but reluctantly I agreed to the nighttime date.

That evening, I rushed our family through dinner so that I could be at the studio at 7:30. When I arrived and walked in, I immediately did not like what I saw; the studio was a small, sterile room with overhead lights, hanging mikes, and a few music stands. There were no windows opening to the outside because the studio needed to be soundproof. The room smelled musty, like a cave in need of fresh air. The walls were covered with old brown carpet and were bare, except for one glass wall looking into the sound engineer's room.

The instrumentalists began arriving and we exchanged pleasantries. I couldn't believe that we were meeting for the first time without a rehearsal, but this was the way they worked. Howard gave them their charts, which were nothing but the time signatures, key signatures, tempos, and chord symbols. I was extra anxious because I had never sung with instrumentalists without having a rehearsal and a detailed music score, plus these were jazz musicians who improvised as they played. "How will I know when to sing?" I asked.

"It's simple. Just watch my eyebrows. When I raise them, that's your cue to begin singing," Howard said.

Oh dear, what a cue that was!

The engineer asked each of us to put on headphones so that we could hear him and the other musicians, and I found them to be uncomfortable and awkward to wear. Then he went into his soundproof room wearing his headphones, manipulating the 4-track soundboard and looking bored.

Another of my problems was that I had no audience. Before when I had sung, I had been able to look into people's eyes and connect with them. Their expressions and faces gave me the encouragement and energy I needed. I fed off of them. Now I was singing for no one but a sound engineer, whom I could only partially see through the glass window. He had an impassive face and sometimes a frown as he fiddled with the controls. *Was my singing okay, or was it bad? How had I let myself get into this mess in this creepy studio with these jazz musicians? Were my songs even fit to be recorded? Would anyone, other than the few in the Friday group and maybe a few friends want to buy the albums? If we didn't sell any, I would be out $2,000 and would have to repay Brigitte for my folly. Was it too late to call off the* *whole project?* My mind was racing.

We were scheduled to record all eleven songs that night, but only recorded three. Between takes we would listen to the recording, and I was disappointed at how my voice sounded. It sounded different from the way I thought it would, and I wasn't sure I liked it or if it was good enough to be recorded. We kept doing take after take, because one of us would make a small mistake and think we could do it better. I pictured the meter running, like watching a taxi meter going up and up. Each time we did another take, I knew it was costing more and more money in studio time, and yet still not sounding any better.

Since we had only competed three songs, we made plans to return the next night. I left feeling discouraged and doubting the outcome.

Then I had an idea for the next session. I asked Jim and a couple of friends to come and be my audience. I needed their ears to listen and their faces to give me encouragement. I no longer needed to watch the engineer's stoic face, but instead looked at my smiling friends. As the time went on, I became more comfortable and relaxed, and my headphones became useful as my second pair of ears. My singing and rapport with the musicians got a little better and we recorded four songs the second night.

When the third night arrived for our last session, I had another idea. I decided to bring beer, thinking it would help us relax and perform better. I had written a song "Jericho," which was based on the Biblical story of the battle when the walls of Jericho came tumbling down. My lyrics said that we all have walls protecting us and they need to come tumbling down. I said "Howard, make the piano sound as if the walls are really falling." He tried several unsuccessful takes and gave up. Then I brought out the beer and after our drinks, conversation, and laughter, he tried one more take. Voila! The walls came tumbling down. We had finally recorded all eleven songs. When we finished, the engineer asked us when we wanted to mix the album. MIX? What was that? I thought we were finished, but now I realized that we would need more studio time and the meter would just keep on ticking and ticking. Howard explained, "We need to come back and listen to the tracks and decide how much of each instrument and how much voice to put into each song." We scheduled a time to mix, and I relied on Howard's ears and musical judgment for the instrumental tracks. After the mix, the recording began to sound better and better, and finally we had the Master tape, which I called "Be Still" ...our first album.

I couldn't believe that we had accomplished such an amazing feat! Beginning with my hearing the woman's voice singing to me, then Brigitte's incredible gift, then sessions with Howard at his house, and finally in the studio, we had recorded an entire album of original songs. In my wildest imagination, I would never have thought of doing such a thing.

Now that the recording was complete, I began to think about the design for the album cover. I consulted with my dearest friend, Mary Beth, who was a gifted artist. Our children were close in age, so our families had spent a lot of time and vacations together. We were both in the Wednesday Prayer Group and in Jim's Friday group. She was like a sister to me and was a strong supporter of my music. Whenever I composed a new song, I would go to her house and play and sing it for her. After Jerry, she was always my first audience and her enthusiasm gave me confidence. We talked about the cover design and she created a lovely drawing of the words, "Be Still" in a soft green monochrome.

That became the front cover but what about the back? I looked at many other record jackets for ideas, and decided to add a black and white photo and bio of me, a bio of the Howard Hanger trio, plus credits to the musicians, artist, and engineer. I asked The Reverend Bud Holland, our associate priest who had gone to the church music conference in Atlanta with me, to write an endorsement on the back cover which I thought would make it more acceptable to church people. Then I wrote these words on the jacket …

God has spoken to us in ancient chants, hymns of the Reformation, and in folksongs and spirituals. God is still speaking to us today through new songs, some of which we can hear deep within ourselves. Perhaps I had never really "listened" before, because until recently, I had never composed a piece of music. Then suddenly and unexpectedly, this music and these words began flowing through me.

Once both sides of the album cover were designed and the soundtrack and copy were ready, I asked Howard how I could find a record company to produce the records and cassettes. He suggested the company that he had used and gave me the contact information. I called them and contracted for five hundred 33 1/3 long playing records, and two hundred cassette tapes. With fear and trepidation, I sent the master tape and album cover design off to Nashville. The days dragged on and on, with no word from the record company. What would happen if the Master was lost? I couldn't even think about what a disaster that would be. I finally got a notice from them that they had received my order and my albums would be ready in three to four weeks.

Those weeks crawled by waiting for the albums to come. I decided to write songbooks and notate them with piano scores and guitar chords, so that others could play and sing the songs. Today all of that notation can be done on the computer, but then it was a painstaking task of writing all the notes by hand on staff paper. It was hard for me, as I was just a medium-skilled pianist who had never written piano scores. Notating was the tedious process of writing down each and every note. I would play a chord or arpeggio and write it note by note. The arpeggios were a bear, as the sixteenth notes ran for two or three octaves. And the rests…was it a quarter rest or an eighth note rest? I sat at the piano day after day, notating the piano score for each song. This was definitely chronos time when the clock ticked slowly on and on.

Next, I had to figure out how to put those scores in a book. I played with paper pages to see how to make a book. It was complicated, because the other half of page one would be the last page of number eighteen or nineteen. I have never been good at details, so this was an effort of discipline and patience. I consulted with Phyllis at the Copy Shop where the pages would be printed, and she helped me get the numbered pages in order. When all the pages were printed, I took them home to collate. Then I took them back to Phyllis to be stapled. Finally, the songbooks were completed and I picked up three shrink-wrapped stacks, each containing 100 songbooks. That was a great relief. It felt like the last day of a school semester when all my papers and exams were completed.

Then the day of reckoning came. Was the initial $2,000 going to cover the cost? I nervously totaled up our expenses. We had spent $325 for the musicians, $400 for the studio, $66 for copyrights, $1016 for the record company, and $28 for the trucking company, which came to the grand total of $1835. Howard's estimate of $2,000 was right on. We even had enough money leftover to pay the copy shop for song sheets and songbooks. We had done it! Now if I could sell the records and cassettes, I would be able to repay Brigitte.

I grew more and more anxious to see and hear the finished product. *What if it didn't sound like it did in the studio? What if the cover looked too home-made? What if my voice sounded weak? How much longer?* I called the record company to see how the production was coming, and they said about another week.

Then, one day, out of the blue a local trucking company called to say that they had several boxes for me. The albums had finally arrived! It was manna from heaven! I dropped everything and with trembling heart and hands, drove to pick them up. Right there in the parking lot, I excitedly tore into the first box. I could hardly believe my eyes. In the square box there was a stack of long-playing albums with beautiful soft green covers, each sealed in cellophane. Then I tore open the rectangular box with its stack of cassette tapes, also individually sealed in cellophane with the same green covers. We had done it! There they were: real albums! *Wow!* I had never even thought of composing a song before. Now here it was... my own album. When I got home I played it over and over and, other than a few minor glitches, I was pleased and proud. Mission accomplished! In 1976 *"Be Still"* was both a record album and a cassette album!

If You Would Ask

If you would ask, I would give you,
On you my blessings, I'd pour.
My love and my power, I would give you,
But you must open the door.

Now that I had these albums, I had to figure out how I was going to share the music and sell them. I sang most every Friday for Jim Goure's group, and they were always appreciative, but they were a small group. How was I going to find larger audiences? About that time, Jim received an invitation to be a speaker at the Spiritual Frontiers Fellowship (SFF) conference in Charlotte. He invited Mary Beth, who painted individual images of people's inner prayers that she called soul paintings, and he invited me with my music to join him. There would be two hundred people there, and I felt that they would be a receptive audience, as SFF is an inclusive, open-minded Christian organization whose members believe in dreams, healing, and meditation. However, I was scared silly, as I didn't know anyone who belonged to the group.

My imagination ran wild as I pictured bead-wearing hippies breaking into chanting and dancing. But my fears were needless, for when I arrived I saw that they were ordinary people like us. We went to the opening meeting, and I was still apprehensive until the moderator opened with the prayer "Almighty God, to whom all hearts are open, all desires known and from whom no secrets are hid." I looked at MaryBeth and we each breathed a sigh of relief because we knew that prayer by heart. We were both Episcopalians and that prayer was from our *Book of Common Prayer.* I did sing several times at the conference and the audience was enthusiastic. Afterwards, many people came up to talk to me and find out where they could buy my music. I happily sent them to the conference bookstore, where my albums and songbooks were on display and was delighted to find out that the store had sold over one hundred albums and songbooks.

My reception in Charlotte had been affirming, but as far as I knew meditation and dream work were not the practices of my fellow parishioners in Trinity Episcopal Church where I was Director of Music. There I kept a low profile about my composing and my spiritual journey. Then one day I decided to talk with my boss, the rector, about my songs. After our weekly staff meeting, I asked if I could speak with him. I said, "I have been writing songs about God and have recently recorded an album of them."

"I've heard about your songs and would like to hear them," he said.

"I've brought you one of the song sheets with all the lyrics" and gave it to him.

As he began to read it, he said, "The words of 'Be Still' in which you say 'You are in the image of me. You are Light, You are Love, You are God' are theologically unsound. God is in us, but we are not God."

I had never thought about theology when I wrote the lyrics but rather the words reflected my personal experiences of God. I knew that the creation story had said that we were made in the image of God, and that Jesus said that the things He did, we could do also. The rector went on to say, "Hymnology should be in the language of a seven-year old child and the word 'essence' is too difficult." I had written, "I am the essence of your being." I disagreed with him, because the next line of my song said "I'm" (meaning God) "nearer than the air you breathe," which explained the word, essence.

He also took me to task for my other songs. "'All He Has is Thee' is almost correct because the rest of the lyrics explain what you mean. Your song 'If You Could But See' only presents one side without the other side, which is to take up your cross. You can't celebrate without recognizing the penitential." The only affirmation I got from him was, "'Jericho' is theologically sound."

I'd expected him to be enthusiastic about my new composing, instead of finding faults and lecturing me about theology. I felt as if I had taken my brand-new baby for him to "ooh" and "aah" over, and instead he was critical and told me that her diaper was smelly. I left our meeting disheartened and discouraged, knowing that my songs would not be suitable for the church.

In spite of my insecurity caused by his criticisms, I knew I would not change them. In my prayers and meditations, I had felt that the words came from the voice of the Holy Spirit speaking deep within me. I was imagining that God was affirming how pleased He was with His creation and His people and that He wanted us to live in the joyful knowledge that He was in us and we were in Him. I could not and would not change the lyrics.

I did get one affirming note from a priest/poet friend, Harry, who said to me, "Poetry is the experience itself. Theology is the reasoned explanation of the experience in looking back, sometimes a generation later. The two do not need to gel." That made sense to me. My music was coming from my experiences of prayer and dreams. I was not trying to be a theologian. Why couldn't my rector understand that and celebrate my new burst of songwriting about God? Instead it felt like Strike One in the game, and I wondered if there would be others.

One morning, I got a call from a woman whom I knew through Jim at the Light Center. She wanted me to come and sing for the Episcopal Church Women (ECW) in her church in High Point. I was thrilled, as this was my first invitation to sing in an Episcopal Church. When the day came, I made the two-hour drive to High Point. I had butterflies because I'd never sung my new songs in a church. I arrived early to have time to go over my music with the church organist, who had agreed to accompany me on the piano. She welcomed me and took me downstairs to the parish hall where the meeting would be. It was in the basement which had a large window that let in some outside light, but it was still a basement. The room for our meeting was ordinary looking with typical institutional folding tables, metal chairs, and a grey linoleum floor. I saw that the women would be seated at the tables for their meeting. When we began rehearsing, I was afraid my piano arrangements would seem simplistic to the organist, but she was gracious and played well. The piano was a little out of tune and missing one key, but was adequate.

Mary Ann, the woman who had invited me, came in with a warm smile and a hug. Then the women began drifting in and finding their seats. Some smiled and some came up to talk with me. When they were all seated, they had a short business meeting and then Mary

Ann introduced me. She said, "I am happy to present Rosemary Crow who is the Director of Music at Trinity Episcopal Church in Asheville. She has composed some songs, and I wanted you to hear her talk about them and sing them." There was a little polite applause, and I rose from my chair and walked over to the piano. I noticed the rector, who must have come in while I was talking with some of the women. He had not bothered to meet me before I began my program and did not sit down, but remained standing leaning against the back wall. He was tall and skinny which made me think of Ichabod Crane, and with his black clericals, looked imposing. As I began talking and singing, he folded his arms across his chest and his face registered an unpleasant scowl. The longer I sang, the more he scowled. From then on, I decided not to look at him but at the women who were listening intently, smiling and nodding. There were about thirty of them and I could feel their favorable response.

When I had finished my songs, he began walking towards me. Other women were approaching me, but he got ahead of them. I wanted to get out of there rather than face him, but I was trapped. Still scowling, he said, "As a priest it is my duty to tell you that your theology is all mixed up." His words cut me deeply and I wanted to run away. As hurt as I was, I steeled myself so that I wouldn't shed a tear. He continued, "You have a beautiful voice and I enjoyed some of your songs, but it is heresy to say, 'You are God' with a capital G. We are not God and all of mankind could not make up God. We are outside of God. God doesn't need us and would not be any less without us."

Once again, it was my song "Be Still" that had upset him... the same song that my own rector had criticized. It was one of my earliest songs and one of my favorites, and based on the words from Isaiah, "Be still and know that I am God." This was the one song for which he had criticized me. Did he even hear the other songs?

I had written the lyrics as if God were speaking to us and saying,

Be still and know I am God.

I am the essence of your being.

I'm nearer than the air you breathe.

Be still and listen to me.

I've come to show you the way.

The way to your divinity.

I've come to set you free.

Be still and listen to me.

You are my beloved, my child.

You are in the image of me.

You are light, You are love. You are God.

Be still and listen to me.

Of all the songs that I had sung, it was the last verse of "Be Still" that had upset him, and I had no comeback. It was the message that the song sang inside of me and I had shared it. I was thinking of what Jesus said in John 14:12. "Very truly, I tell you, the one who believes in me will also do the works that I do; and , in fact, will do greater works than these." I also remembered my clergy friend, Harry, telling me about the difference between poetry and theology. I clearly knew that I was not quoting the voice of God, but I was writing the words that I imagined God might be saying to us. I absolutely knew that I was a poet and not a theologian!

However, when the rector challenged me, I was tongue-tied and couldn't remember any of those things. He went on and on, and I felt smaller and smaller. He said that he could never invite me to preach in his church because of my strange theology. As I silently stood there, I did smile to myself as I thought, *But today I have already preached in your church.* He ended by saying "You may be right and I may be wrong," which was not helpful.

My heart was pounding, and I didn't respond. How could I argue theology with a priest? All I did was nod my head and say, "I'm sorry that you did not like my songs."

About that time, a woman came up and took him to task and I backed away and let them have at it. Many of the women came up and spoke to me to let me know how much they had enjoyed my songs. Their words were heart-warming, but I left with a sinking feeling, knowing that my songs were not suitable for a traditional church. I also knew that the rector's brother was the rector of an Episcopal church in Black Mountain where our Bishop lived. That might mean that I would never be singing in our Diocese. Strike Two!

Then something wonderful happened. A parishioner invited me to sing in my own church for the Trinity Episcopal Church Women's luncheon. Could I risk it? Would that be my third strike? Bishop Weinhauer would be the speaker, and even though I would only sing two songs, how would he react? As our Bishop, he had the voice of authority in our diocese. An affirmation from him would carry great weight, but a negative reaction would be the kiss of death for ever being invited to sing in Episcopal churches. Had he already heard a negative report from the brother of the High Point priest about my singing in his church? Plus, it's always difficult to sing for those who know you best; these women were my friends, some of whom were in my choir. Many did not even know I was composing. In spite of those negatives, I decided to risk it and sing.

The day of the luncheon arrived, and I was filled with anxiety. I knew each of the sixty or so women who came and wondered how I would be received, but mostly I worried about the Bishop's reaction. My stomach was churning so I couldn't eat any of my lunch. When it was time for me to sing, I did. Then Bishop Weinhauer stood up to speak. My heart was pounding. What would he say? He began his talk by saying that he had recently been to a conference in Houston where Betty Pulkingham spoke about her outpouring of new songs. She was the choirmaster at a large Episcopal Church where her husband was a priest. The Bishop quoted her saying, "An anointing for new songs had come to rest upon a body of believers. The first song was the lock that opened the dam and let the waters of creativity roll in." Then he said, "Today, I think we have listened to another gift from the Holy Spirit in Rosemary's music. Thank you, Rosemary."

I couldn't believe my ears. He understood! This was a gold star from the top… from our Bishop. Maybe my music would be received by the church after all. This felt like a Home Run and maybe there would be no Strike Three.

Like Betty's experiences at the Episcopal church in Houston, my personal dam had burst and the songs kept rolling in. There were forty-one new songs now, so I felt I was ready to record another album. I had the money from the sales of records, cassettes, and books from the Light Center and the SFF conference and I finally had the joy of repaying Brigitte her two thousand dollars!

In the Stillness is the Dancing

In the Stillness is the Dancing.
In the Silence is the Singing.
In the Stillness is Creation.
That is the mystery.

My special tree outside the window across from my piano was continuing to vibrate with music when I wrote "In the Stillness." It was inspired by the image of the energy swirling in the eye of the storm, which was meaningful to me because of the many hurricanes I had experienced as a child growing up in south Florida. As children, we were too innocent to be frightened. Rather, an approaching hurricane meant that my dad, along with our friends' dads would be away, because they were commercial pilots whose job was to fly the planes out of harm's way. Then we knew that two or three moms with their kids would stay together for a couple of days, which was one big party for us kids. My memory of hurricanes is that first the wind would blow fiercely from one direction. The windows and doors would shake and the storm would roar. Then, all of a sudden, there would be total silence. It was not a passive silence, but an intense silence filled with such power and energy that I could feel it. For a minute or two the storm would stop and sometimes we even saw sunshine. When that happened, I begged my mother to let me go outside, but she said, "No. It is too dangerous as you never know when the fierce wind will start again, only this time from the other direction." Still, I had longed to go outside and touch and be touched by this strong and mysterious silence. I named the second album "In the Stillness is the Dancing."

Since Bishop Weinhauer had appreciated and endorsed my music, I asked him to write on the new album cover. He wrote "Often, I thought I detected the echo of an ancient psalmist being heard in modern song." Now I felt officially blessed by the church. Once again, my dear artist friend, Mary Beth designed the cover with a stylized drawing of the winds around the eye of the storm with birds circling in the calm. My words on the cover read:

God is the eye—that stillness in the center of life's hurricane. The confusions, problems, noises, and sheer busyness of living surround us and threaten to destroy.

Yet, in the eye of the storm, we can find that same charged stillness, that same dynamic quiet.

I called Howard about recording a new album, and he said he was ready to go again. He knew about a larger 8-track studio that we could use this time with a professional sound engineer. We expanded with more instruments—an oboe, two trumpets, a trombone, percussion, string quartette, and even a tin whistle for my children's song, "Thank you God." I asked some singers from my Trinity Children's Choir to sing it on the album. It was delightful to have those twelve young, enthusiastic voices, and it was a special joy that Leslie, our daughter, was among them. This time the process was familiar, and the new recording studio was bright and more inviting.

Once again, we did it!

We recorded twelve original songs and I sent the finished Master and the copy for the album off to Nashville, ordering 500 albums and 500 cassettes. Once again, I completed the laborious task of notation for the songbooks. Finally, the finished product arrived, and in 1978 our second album was birthed, "In the Stillness is the Dancing." The cover was lively with the photo of the twelve singing choir children. I was ecstatic to have completed a second record and cassette album of my songs!

The songs kept pouring out—usually inspired by my dreams, meditations, prayer group, and Jim's lectures. However in this joyous burst of creativity, a dark cloud was looming. Our son, Sam had scoliosis and the curve in his spine was worsening. We took him to our local orthopedist, then went to our first chiropractor, and finally to Shriners Hospital in Greenville. Each doctor advised us, "Wait and see," as Sam was still growing. Even though he was only fifteen years old, he was already 6'3" tall. They agreed that he might need a body brace for a couple of years, and in a worst-case scenario, surgery.

Meanwhile I was carrying on with my job as Director of Music at Trinity, but my heart was in noodling on the piano and listening for new songs. Jim asked me to write a chant for peace for the upcoming Light Center Advance. He called these events advances rather than retreats. The next time I noodled I heard a chant. It sounded so familiar. Was it truly original? That question often came up as I composed a song. Was it really new, or was it a tune from a song already known? Since this was a recurring question for me, I frequently played and sang my new songs for friends and asked them if they had ever heard the melody. If they said no, I was assured that it was a new song. The chant I wrote for the advance was a round in three parts. When I introduced it that night, people caught on quickly and sang all three parts. How wonderful it was to hear the song come alive as they sang it in harmony!

I had several musical adventures with Jim. Once he was invited by the Unity Church in Kingston, Jamaica to come and present his message on "Effective Prayer." He also had invitations to speak in Florida, so he decided to drive and speak in churches along the way, and then fly to Jamaica from Miami. He invited me to join him along with his wife, Diana, to sing my music. At first, I was hesitant about going on a trip out of the country, but Jerry was supportive of my going, so I prayed about it and in my heart, I heard a loud YES. I'll never forget singing in the Unity Church in Kingston. It was a large, white, round sanctuary. There were open windows all the way around with the brilliant tropical sun streaming in. The church was overflowing so that some of the people had to sit in the open windows. The congregants' bright smiles lit up the room. They sang the hymns with such rhythm and gusto, and when I sang my song, "Shine" with its Calypso rhythm, the church was rocking! It was a glorious experience for me.

Another memorable trip was when I went with Jim and his wife to Memphis to visit famous soprano, Marguerite Piazza. She and her husband, Harry, had asked Jim to come and speak about Effective Prayer to some of their friends. Again, he invited me to join them and sing my songs. SING?? Sing for Marguerite Piazza? I knew that she was a diva who had sung with the Metropolitan Opera; I remembered seeing her several times on television and hearing her vibrant operatic voice. Even though I felt inadequate, I decided to go because it was such a fantastic opportunity to meet her.

We drove to Memphis and when we arrived, she graciously met us at the door. She definitely looked the part of a grande dame, elegantly dressed and dripping with diamonds and pearls. Her thick hair was dyed jet black, and her face almost white with caked powder. She invited us in and after we sat down, she said that she would like to give me a voice lesson and had arranged for her accompanist to come over and accompany me. I was terrified as I could barely find the courage to even talk with her. How was I ever going to sing for her? What song would I sing? All I had in my repertoire were my own songs.

The time came and her accompanist arrived. We went into her studio with the beautiful ebony grand piano. She began by having me sing some vocal exercises. These made me stretch my vocal range higher and higher. Then she asked, or rather commanded, me to sing a high C. I was terrified, but I took a deep breath, closed my eyes, and somehow or other, I sang it. Then I think I sang some of my songs for her, but after the high C, that's all I remember. That evening, she gave a lovely dinner party and four couples came all dressed to the nines. After dinner, she asked Jim to speak and me to sing. I sang "Be Still" and two other songs. Her guests were eager to hear Jim and graciously listened to me. I'll never forget that visit.

That summer, Jim was invited to speak at another SFF conference at a college in St. Albion, Michigan, and again this time he asked Mary Beth with her soul paintings, and me with my music to go with him. I would speak and sing, and it would be an opportunity to sell my albums. I had confidence singing my songs and speaking about them because Jim and I had been so well received at the SFF conference in Charlotte. It was also like a mini-vacation to go with Jim and my best friend, Mary Beth.

The first evening we did our three-part gig with Jim's talk, Mary Beth's art, and my singing for an appreciative audience. Mary Beth and I always had a laugh when we were on the same program, because invariably someone from the audience would come up to talk with us and would call her Rosemary and call me Mary Beth. The funny part was that we were opposites in appearance. She was ten years older than I and her blonde hair was pulled back in a bun, while I had short black hair in a pixie cut. Through the years, when people mixed us up, rather than correct them we just answered to either name, which was a little joke between us.

After our program, I took a long walk by myself around the college campus. It was a beautiful summer evening and with daylight savings time it was only dusk, even though it was almost nine o'clock. I wanted to think about all that had happened since my composing began and reflect on where it was taking me. When I finished my walk, I found my way to the room where Mary Beth and I were staying. It was a typical college dorm room with twin beds and twin desks. After talking awhile, we both settled down to sleep, and then I had an amazing dream about a twelve-year old boy. He was standing in front of a group of people in a church and was reading Psalm 108 aloud. When I woke up, I looked for a Bible in the room, but there was not one there. I had no idea what Psalm 108 was about. I hoped it wouldn't be about lamentations or wars, and prayed that it would have a message for me. I remembered from my walk the night before that I had passed the college bookstore. Surely I could find a Bible there.

We got dressed and went to breakfast, and then I went to find the bookstore. It was open and I went in and found the religion section. I took a Bible from the shelf and with an anxious heart and trembling hands I opened it to Psalm 108. I was overwhelmed with the words. I wanted to shout it out to the customers in the bookstore. It seemed to be a message just meant for me. It said, *"My heart is ready, O God! I will sing and make melody. I will give thanks to thee, O Lord among the peoples."*

Deep within, I knew that this was an affirmation from God. That morning right there in the college bookstore, I made a covenant with God. I promised that from then on, I would sing and stand strong. I would sing and speak the truth as I understood it, no matter who was listening or criticizing my words.

Soon after I returned from Michigan, we had "Deaf Awareness Sunday" at Trinity. For many years, our deaf congregation had met on Sundays in the undercroft and sometimes joined the regular congregation for special services. That Sunday, our Diocesan Minster for the Deaf was the preacher. About 30 deaf members sat in the first three pews and signed the hymns and prayers. Since I was in the choir in the front of the church, I could see them clearly and was deeply moved by their signing. It was as if their fingers were dancing. That night I wrote the song "Singing/Signing" from the point of view of a deaf person. I was intrigued by the fact that the spelling for singing was the same as for signing, with two letters reversed. The lyrics said,

You are singing. We are signing, as we worship here with you.
May your eyes hear, as our hands share, our world of silence with you.
As your voices join in singing in God's holy house of prayer.
So our fingers join in dancing. The Word of God fills the air.

When the Wood is Split

When the wood is split,
When the tree is broken,
When the wood is split,
I am there. I am there.

Our personal storm was growing as our son, Sam's curve on his spine was increasing. Sam was an extremely tall fifteen-year old who loved golf and basketball. It was his freshman year in high school, and he was on the golf team and looking forward to being on the varsity basketball team the next year. Once again, we made the round of doctors' appointments, and the doctors at Shriners Hospital in Greenville, South Carolina, along with two Asheville surgeons, agreed that surgery was now inevitable. I again took Sam to the chiropractor and to Jim's for healing lights, but nothing was stopping his curve from progressing. Sam agreed that he should go ahead and have the surgery, and we were relieved that it was also his decision. Jerry researched the best surgeon for scoliosis and found Dr Hugo Keim at Columbia Presbyterian Hospital in New York City. He called in May for an appointment, and Dr Keim said that he had just had a cancellation for surgery on Friday, June 13th, because of a patient's superstition. We were grateful for that and took it as a good omen.

In May, Sam and Jerry flew up and met with Dr Keim. He scheduled Sam for surgery on June 13th with pre-surgery arrangements to begin on June 6th. Meanwhile at home, our lives went full speed ahead. Our daughter, Leslie had to have an emergency appendectomy, and my church responsibilities were compounded with Pentecost and Trinity Sunday approaching. We had the final performance of the youth handbell choir, the opera "Joseph and His Technicolor Dreamcoat" by the children's choir, and a year-end trip. That year I'd wanted to go on a picnic and hike to celebrate our choir season, but the children outvoted me and Ghost Town, a local tourist attraction, it was. After that, before we could even catch our breath, June 6th had arrived.

Sam and I flew to New York City on June 6th for his many pre-surgery procedures and the beginning fittings of his body cast. When they put him in his first cast, it was too tight and caused him indigestion, pain, and finally vomiting. I tearfully pleaded with the nurses for help, and finally a doctor came and cut a small section of his cast away to relieve the pressure on his abdomen. As the days went on, Sam's body began to adjust to the cast and he was feeling better and able to eat more. On June 12th, the day before his surgery, Jerry and Leslie flew up. We both perked up when they appeared. Even though we were in the depths of despair, they lifted our spirits.

The surgery was early the next morning and was successful, but Sam ended up being in the hospital for five long, difficult weeks, even though we had only expected him to be there for three. There were complications—his wound was very slow in healing. Through it all, Sam was courageous and strong and endured much pain and suffering. It was a horrendous experience for all of us. As his mother,

I felt completely helpless, and I was angry at God. I was consumed with the question…*Why? Why did this happen to our fine, young son?* I was unable to pray or to feel the presence of God. I had one opportunity to vent my anger when we first checked into the hospital and I filled out our forms. One of the blanks asked what my religion was, and I defiantly wrote NONE.

Through the long post-operative weeks, I began to learn how much I needed love and caring from our friends. Their phone calls and cards meant so much. Even the people in the hospital who had once been strangers ministered to us. There was George, whose daughter was having the same surgery. He was a short, fat, Jewish man with a heavy accent, and he made Sam laugh. He came every day and brought Sam sports magazines and told him jokes. There was Pat, a patient about my age who had scoliosis surgery the week before Sam. Her outcome was not successful because her legs ended up being paralyzed, and yet her courage and kindness ministered to me. There was Phoebe, a young beautiful nurse from the islands who spoke with a lilting calypso accent. One day, when she saw me in tears, she came and put her arms around me and held me while I cried.

I was deeply wounded during this time, and for the first time I began to learn what compassion was all about and how much it meant for all those people to reach out to us. This inspired my song "People."

> *God was in the people, the people, the ones who called His name.*
> *Yes, God was in the people, through them His Spirit came,*
> *The ones who called his name.*

Finally on July 11th, Sam was released from the hospital and we were able to go home. Jerry's law partner had arranged for a client's pilot to come up in his small plane and fly us back home. The space in the plane enabled Sam, who was in his body cast, to lie down on the back seat. We took off and watched the city fade away to a blue sky and white clouds. After a couple of hours, we began to descend. As our plane circled over the mountains, we saw Asheville; it had never looked so good! Having been surrounded by high rises, cement sidewalks, and the cacophony of the 24/7 ambulances at the hospital, our home in the woods was our sanctuary, surrounded by green trees, lush flowers, and blessed quiet. Jerry and Leslie met us at the airport and we were glad to be a family again. When we got home, our dog Misty covered Sam with kisses. We set Sam up on the sofa bed in the den so that he wouldn't have to climb stairs. He was weak and uncomfortable, but we were home!

We had been tossed and turned by the storm, living one day at a time. It took me about a month before I could find my peaceful, constant place in the eye of the hurricane, and get back into the groove of stillness and silence. But I was still feeling angry. Before the surgery when Sam' scoliosis was getting worse, I believed that if I had faith and trusted enough, he would be healed. It was hard giving up that concept and realizing that his surgery was inevitable. Gradually I began to realize that God had, in fact, been with us each step of the way, beginning with guiding us to Dr. Keim who was the best scoliosis surgeon. This was confirmed when his picture appeared on the cover of TIME magazine the week after Sam's surgery. In Columbia-Presbyterian Hospital, Sam had the excellent care that he needed because of his post-surgery complications. Even though I had tried to shut God out, He had found a way to slip in through other people.

After many months, I was able to be grateful to God and to realize that He had been with us in the hospital, in the patients and nurses, and in our family and friends.

That fall, I was invited to join a group and enroll in a course called TEE (Theological Education by Extension) formulated by The School of Theology in Sewanee, TN. There were ten of us, and we met one evening a week in the home of our mentor Richard, who was a young priest. The course encouraged questions and soul searching, and I began to wrestle with my own personal theology. I had thought the church too rigid for me and yet Jim and his New Age teachings were also rigid. As we studied the Bible and church history, I began to see that theology was not as cut and dried as I had thought. There seemed to be a space for questions and doubts…granted that that was only a minority point of view, but church history confirmed that there had always been questioners and doubters just like me.

I was wondering where I belonged. One Friday morning, I went to the Light Center for our regular Friday group. For the first time, I felt uncomfortable and out of place. The meeting started and Jim stood and began his lecture. I was sitting facing the glass door that opened to the outside. I kept looking at the sign over the door that said EXIT, and it seemed to be bright and vibrating as if it were speaking to me. The thought came loud and clear that it was time for me to leave the Light Center. I was no longer in sync with Jim's message, which was authoritative and left no wiggle room. I needed to stand on my own two feet and speak the truth as I perceived it—not Jim's truth, but mine. He had said that we should not question God. Well, I was full of doubts, and God was the main one I needed to question. This led me to compose my song,

"Questions." The lyrics said,

The people who have all the answers, don't really understand the questions.

And the people who understand the questions are always searching for the answers.

I asked Jim to meet with me after the meeting and told him what I was feeling. It was painful for both of us when I told him that I needed to leave the Friday group. We both had tears in our eyes as he said, "You've gotten the message. Now go."

My heart was churning. Was I doing the right thing in closing the door on the Friday group and the Light Center? After all, this was where my music had begun. If I left, would I still hear the music? And yet I had the strong inner knowing that it was time for me to leave.

Enter the Silence

Enter the Silence deep in the heart of God.
Deep in the Silence a still small voice is heard.
Sweet, mystic Silence gathers and magnifies
In one small Word.

I felt that the Holy Spirit was guiding me with my compositions. Like the time I wanted to write a hymn for the Earth, based on the words of the Saint Francis Prayer. I couldn't remember all the words and I needed another verse. I looked in books that I had around the house, but couldn't find the text. This was before the age of computers and searching Google. That morning, Sam came downstairs and said he needed to take a book of poetry to school for his English class. I can't even remember what he was looking for, but I did find a book for him. Before I gave it to him, it fell open and there was the Saint Francis Prayer with the verse I needed. It was another wonderful gift of synchronicity that made me smile.

I had written so many new songs that I was already thinking about a third album. I wanted the album to be joyful and have an upbeat sound. I fantasized about having a small group of singers like a folk singing group, singing songs of joy and peace. How was I going to find them? I couldn't select some from my choir as it might cause hard feelings to choose only a few. One night, out of the blue, a friend called and said, "There are eight of us in a singing group...two sopranos, two altos, two tenors and two basses and we can't find any music. Do you have any suggestions for us?"

I laughed and said, "Do I ever!" I met with them that week and knew that this was the group I had been imagining. I arranged some of the songs for four-parts, and we began rehearsing until they were ready to sing them on our new album "Holy Silence."

I called Howard to ask him once again to help me with an album and he said, "Yes." After several sessions of working with him on instrumental arrangements, we were ready to record. This time we went to the same engineer who had recently built a new 16-track studio in his house in West Asheville. It was bright and welcoming, and I was now more comfortable with the recording process. It was especially enjoyable to have these enthusiastic singers who were also my friends. We added a cello, flute, and English horn to our previous instruments of piano, violins, viola, oboe, guitar and bass. The recording went smoothly and only took three sessions. Then we mixed it, and it was complete. Once again Mary Beth designed the album cover, and I asked my friend, the Rev. Harry Woggon and Jim to write on the back. I also wrote and said,

Just three years ago on my birthday, I received a beautiful gift. I heard the song "Holy Silence" singing deep within me, and now it is the title song for this third album. This music from the Holy Spirit has been singing within me ever since. In the Holy Silence that is deep within us and all around us, we can each listen with our inner ears.

I sent the master tape and copy off to the record processing company, ordering 500 record albums and 300 cassette tapes. And once again, I laboriously notated the accompanying songbooks and ordered 300 of them from the printer. When the new albums, "Holy Silence" finally came by truck, I wanted to celebrate. This was a new creation, and I needed a way to share it with others. I wondered if it would be possible for me to give a concert at Trinity with Howard and the other musicians? Howard thought that was a good idea and we engaged Eli on bass and Beth on violin and vocal harmonies. After checking with the rector and the church calendar, we agreed on a date. When all our plans were finalized, I sent flyers and invitations to everyone I knew.

The afternoon before the concert, Howard, the musicians, and I met at the church to rehearse. We decided what order we would perform my songs and what would be the first song. Howard said, "Choose an upbeat, rhythmic song to open. Enter singing that song and afterwards you can speak and welcome the people." I thought my calypso-rhythmic song, "Shine" would fit the bill.

When we had finished rehearsing our planned program, I told Howard that I had written a new song and I thought that if the audience gave us an encore, we could perform it. I sang and played it and Howard liked it, so we agreed to keep it in reserve. The song was "Weave," and was inspired by our new rector, Grahame Butler-Nixon, who had just come to us from Australia the Sunday before. In his sermon that first Sunday, he had said that he knew that God had called him to us and us to him, and he was eagerly waiting to see how God would weave our lives together. When I got home from church and began to noodle, the song "Weave" came in full-blown.

After our rehearsal, I went home to rest and then to put on my fancy black dress that I had bought for just that occasion. I needed to eat a light supper but could hardly eat anything because I was so excited and nervous. My stomach was churning with butterflies, or something larger... like birds! I was the first one to arrive at the church and opened the door with my key. It was eerie to enter into the large, silent sanctuary, but soon Howard and the musicians came in.

After a little while, I began to hear noise and conversations as people began to arrive. I cracked the door and peeked out. I was thrilled to see how many friends had come, but that also make it especially scary since I knew them all. Finally, it was 8 o'clock and the three musicians made their way onto the stage, which was the raised area in front of the altar. When they began playing my song, "Shine," all my fears vanished. Howard was smiling and when he raised his eyebrows, that was my cue to walk out and begin singing. From then on, the evening was absolute joy for me. It was exhilarating to perform my own music with live musicians! I had always loved performing and receiving the energy from the audience, but this time it was over the top!

I couldn't keep from looking at the musicians while I was singing; it was as if we had a secret communication between us. When I saw Howard's tongue slide out of his mouth onto his left lower lip, I knew he was totally absorbed in the music, and it meant we were all in sync. I could have sung all night, but the concert went by in the blink of an eye. It was truly Kairos time. The audience clapped and clapped for an encore. Once again, Howard raised his eyebrows, which was our cue to play and sing "Weave." The people's response was immediate. They were already standing and clapping and when I began singing, they began to sway and sing as if they had always known the chorus. We instantly *knew* that "Weave" was a powerful song that was inviting, joyful and singable.

Afterwards at the reception, it was good to talk with different friends and hear their comments about the evening. Mary Beth had a table set up with my records, cassettes, and songbooks, and she made over one hundred and fifty sales.

There's a Star

There's a Star, shining bright.
I never saw it before tonight.
Such a Star. What does it mean?
If I should follow it, where would it lead?

A few months later, a Methodist minister in Rock Hill called to ask if I could come and lead a three-night revival at his church. He said, "I've quoted some of your songs in my sermons, and my congregation would enjoy hearing you in person."

I was floored to hear this, and said, "I've never even been to a Revival."

He said, "It will be more of rededication, like a renewal."

"I'll be happy to speak and sing for the renewal part, but you will need to lead the reviving!"

About that time Madeleine L'Engle came to Trinity and spoke on creativity. She was a great "Shero" (a female hero) to me as I had read all her books and was in sync with her thoughts about God and creativity. I was lucky to have some private time with her because she and my rector, Grahame, were long-time friends. At first I was silent and in awe of her, but when I got over my nervousness, I told her about my invitation to the renewal and my reluctance to accept. She said "Go. Don't ever turn down an invitation as you never know what it will bring." I took her words to heart as my marching orders and I began to have the wild idea that I would love to do what she did: lead retreats and speak in churches, and I could share my music. But I wondered if I had enough to sing and say? Then there was the basic question of would I ever be invited? I remembered Fred Buechner saying, "Vocation is the place where your great joy meets the world's great hunger." I wasn't sure that my music would meet the world's hunger, but I did know that it was my great joy.

However, even my joy in composing had its own setbacks. I began a new project of composing music for Rite C in the *Episcopal Book of Common Prayer*. I called it "Mass of Covenant" because of my covenant with God, as I remembered the vivid dream I had had when I was singing in Michigan. I loved Rite C with its images of "the vast expanse of interstellar space, galaxies, suns, the planets in their courses, and this fragile earth our island home." The melodies I wrote were sometimes jazzy and sometimes seemed to echo ancient Jewish-sounding songs. I composed music for the Gloria in Excelsis, the Lord's Prayer, the Sursum Corda, and the Sanctus and Benedictus. I set all the Celebrant's words to a chant, so that the entire Mass could be sung. Our organist, Mark Jones wrote the organ score, and I was excited and eager to present it to Grahame and to Trinity thinking, that they would be as enthusiastic as I was about my musical setting of the Mass.

A Liturgical Committee meeting was scheduled for the next week to plan Holy Week, Easter, and Pentecost. When I enthusiastically told them about my creation and asked if we could sing it for Pentecost, I was crushed by their negative reaction. They said that the people would not be able to sing a new musical setting because it would be too difficult. I couldn't believe what I was hearing. They were not welcoming my new music, but instead they were resistant. Why weren't they glad that I had written this new arrangement? I explained that the choir would learn the music and lead the singing, and the music would be printed in the bulletins for the congregation to sing.

Grahame let them vent all their bad feelings and then he put it to a vote, which he worded in such a way that it would be hard for them to say no. They reluctantly voted yes, and it was scheduled for Pentecost. I was relieved about that, but left the meeting feeling hurt and angry. When Pentecost came, we did sing my Mass of Covenant. The choir sang it well, the congregation joined in, and Grahame beautifully chanted. It was heart-warming to hear it sung by the choir and congregation, but the experience for me was bittersweet. I had the nagging thought that I would never hear it sung again. That has come true. I do hope that one day a choir will learn and sing it, and that I'll be there to hear it.

I began to think more and more about resigning from my job as Trinity's Director of Music, and I wondered if it would be possible to take a six-month leave to try out my new venture? I thought that while I was away Jenni, my assistant, could take over directing the choir. Then if it didn't work out, I could resume my position. I planned to speak with Grahame after Tuesday's staff meeting. We met in the Rector's office, which was a warm and inviting room with wood-paneled walls and comfortable chairs. Behind his desk there was a large window where the morning sun flooded in and we could see the great old elm tree outside. For thirteen years, I had sat in the same chair meeting with the staff: our Rector, Associate Rector, Administrative Secretary, Secretary, the Director of Children's

Ministries, the Sexton, and me, the Director of Music. I remembered back to those first years when Leslie was just a young child and I had brought her with me to the meetings. She would sit on the floor beside me, play with her Barbies, and sometimes eat a banana. Our Rector seemed to enjoy having her there. Now it was years later, and Grahame was our new Rector.

I spoke to him just before our meeting and told him that I would like to talk with him privately afterwards. During the meeting, I began to have doubts. What if I resigned from Trinity and was not invited anywhere to sing? What if Grahame didn't like my idea of a six-month trial run? Maybe I should wait a little longer and be sure that invitations were beginning to come. During our meeting we heard the phone ring, and the other church secretary who did not come to the meetings, answered the phone. She came into our meeting and said, "There's a long-distance phone call for Rosemary." That was long before the time of cell phones: long-distance calls were special. On the phone, a priest in Charlotte was calling to ask if I could come to his church on a Sunday in September.

That was just the nudge I needed. Afterwards when Grahame and I talked, he said, "It needs to be a clean break and not a six-months' leave. You can't hold on with one hand while you try out your new venture. It wouldn't be fair to the choir, or to Jenni." I felt like I was standing on a diving board not knowing whether to dive in or climb back down the ladder when Grahame came up behind me and gave me a push. Suddenly I was swimming in deep water trying to catch my breath and kicking, even though I had no idea where I was going.

Anxiety about my resignation, with many doubts and questions kept nagging me. It was scary giving up my position that I had enjoyed at Trinity, plus my monthly paycheck. *What if no one invited me to come and sing?* I was closing the door behind me without any certainty of what lay ahead. Yet deep in my heart I knew it was the right thing to do.

I planned to tell the choir about my decision to resign when we met the next Thursday at our weekly practice. When I told them, I surprised myself by bursting into tears, as did three of my favorite singers. A few weeks later, when the date came for my last Sunday, I was filled with sadness as I led the choir and looked into each of their faces. There was Sally, our oldest member with her sweet voice, and her daughter, Sue, who usually sang sour notes. There was old Joe, who many times complained about my choice of music, and there was dear Mark, our organist, who always supported me. After the service, we recessed down the aisle and out of the church. I went into the choir dressing room, took off my choir robe and with a deep sigh, hung it in the closet. That was my swan song as Choir Director. On the first of September, 1982, after 13 years, I had resigned from my job as Director of Music at Trinity Parish. I felt a sense of loss, but also excited and more than anxious about the future.

I was still wondering where my next direction would take me, and I began trying out different venues. I enrolled in Western Carolina University to begin working on my Master's in Counseling. I also began leading the Trinity Women's Bible weekly meetings, took Hospice training, and organized a new Education for Ministry group that I would mentor. I was even considering applying for Deacon's training. I was floundering in many different directions, thinking that if my music didn't work out, maybe one of these would emerge as the path for me.

I began having powerful dreams and I wanted to understand their meaning. Through friends, I found out about a Jungian analyst who lived about an hour away in Pea Ridge, North Carolina. I called her and made an appointment. I had never gone to a therapist and didn't know what to expect. I anxiously drove down the mountain, and wondered if she would be pushy and threatening, or a little crazy, or maybe not any help at all? I pulled into the driveway of her small mountain cottage. My stomach was in knots as I rang the doorbell.

She opened the door and greeted me with a big smile. She was a white-haired woman who appeared both sensible and practical. After that first session, I continued to work with her for several months, telling her about my dreams. She helped me understand that I was searching for my own inner authority—not from the church and not from Jim's group—but from within. I remembered my dream about the twelve-year old boy reading Psalm108 which said, "My heart is ready, O God, my heart is ready! I will sing and make melody." It was that dream that compelled me to make a covenant with God to sing and to speak my own truth, but how and where? I wanted to be more than a performer, but rather a proclaimer speaking and singing what my inner self was shouting.

That fall after my Trinity resignation, I only had four invitations. The first was to the Revival at the Methodist Church in Rock Hill where Madeleine L'Engle had urged me to go, and one to a Presbyterian Church in Salisbury. Another was due to my phone call from the priest in Charlotte who had given me the courage to resign. He had invited me to give a program for his parish that was having a weekend retreat at Kanuga, which is an Episcopal Conference Center in Hendersonville. The fourth one was an invitation also at Kanuga, to sing at the Medicine and Ministry Conference.

At that conference, one of the attendees gave me the idea for what would become one of my favorite songs, "The Gift of Presence." We were in a small group talking when a man opened his heart and shared with us all the losses and griefs that he was carrying. When he finished talking, we were all silent, not knowing how to respond. Finally, someone said that all we could offer and all we had to give one another was our gift of presence. That night I wrote the song, "The Gift of Presence," which has been meaningful to many people. I had the card printed with the words and still send it to someone who is grieving. The cards say,

The gift of presence is what I offer you.
A holy meeting between us two.
I have no answers, but I can share
My gift of presence with you.

I was learning to listen as ideas for songs came from many sources, and sometimes from requests. I wrote a baptismal song for our friends' new baby girl, Erika, and sang it at her Baptism at Warren Willson Chapel. The song begins,

Dear little baby, shining and bright,
dwelling within you God's holy light.
Innocent baby, Bearer of truth.
Help us remember now what we once knew.

I was also working on an instrumental song cycle to go with the seven colors of healing lights in Jim's Light Center which I had promised him last year. Sometimes, in my composing, I would begin with the words, like in my song "Go In Peace," which was based on the blessing that our Rector gave at the close of each morning service at Trinity, and another song "Truly," which was based on a poem by the Rev. Harry Woggon.

Now that I had so many new songs, I began thinking about creating another album. I called Howard and once more, he agreed to help. I always looked forward to our collaborations. The process of arranging my songs with him was the most enjoyable part of the whole recording scenario. He was excited about his new synthesizer that he wanted to use on the album. Robert Moog, the inventor of the synthesizer lived in Asheville, and Howard had worked with him. I, on the other hand, was opposed to any electronic sounds. I wanted real instruments played by live, in the flesh, instrumentalists. But Howard was persuasive so I agreed that he could play it on one song, but only on that one! Later, I had to admit how much I liked the sound that Howard had created, which sounded like an angelic choir in my song "Enter the Silence." The words are,

Enter the silence, deep in the heart of God.
Deep in the silence a still, small voice is heard.
Sweet mystic silence gathers and magnifies
In one, small word.

Not all the songs were angelic. When I played another new song for him, "You are the Light of the World," he laughed out loud and said, "Rosemary, you've written a country song,"

I was horrified. "Oh, no. I don't even like country."

"The chords and rhythmic structure are pure country."

"Could you at least make it sophisticated country?"

He added some syncopation that disguised the square rhythm just a little. This song became a crowd favorite. Whenever I sang it, I would look at the audience and choose someone's name. Then, when I sang the words, "You are the Light of the World," I would insert the person's name for the word You. That was always a hit!

We were finally ready to record our fourth album, "Go in Peace." We went to our same engineer, who was now downtown in a new 32-track studio. With more tracks, we added more instruments which included Howard's piano and the synthesizer, plus a string quartet of violin, viola, cello and bass as well as a flugelhorn, guitar, and percussion. First we laid down the rhythm track with guitar, percussion, and bass; next the string quartet and any solo instruments, and finally the vocals. I was not as stressed out as I had been in earlier recordings and enjoyed the creative process. The string players took up the most time as they were never satisfied with their playing and wanted to do take after take, until mindful of the accumulating costs, I finally had to say, "No more!"

Howard laughed. "They can even hear the grass growing."

I was thrilled that Madeleine L'Engle agreed to write on this album jacket, and also Grahame. My cover notes began with my song "Journey", which said,

Come and go with me. I will lead you home.
Even through the wilderness, I will bring you home.
Throughout the ages, God has called his people into covenant.
God is still calling us, his people into covenant.
God has given me the gift of song and called me to share it.
This album is a tangible sigh of the direction that God is calling me.

When the album was completed in 1982, we decided to give another concert at Trinity. Seeing so many friends in the audience and singing with Howard and his musicians once again was thrilling. When I had the opportunity to sing with live musicians, it was exciting, electric… an out-of-body experience. One of the highlights that night was afterwards at the reception when I had a conversation with my former rector. He was the one who had criticized the lyrics in my early song, "Be Still."

"Rosemary," he said, "I didn't understand why you had resigned. I thought that being Minister of Music at Trinity should be enough. But after tonight I understand. You truly have a Music Ministry." His validation was one that I had been waiting a long time to hear! He confirmed what I knew on a deep level. I was on the right path, doing what I was meant to be doing… composing and singing my music.

Weave

A moment ago, still we did not know
Our unity, only diversity.
Now the Christ in me greets the Christ in thee,
In one great family.
Weave, Weave, Weave us together.
Weave us together in unity and love.

Weave was beginning to have a life of its own, as I was getting calls from people all over the country who were requesting permission to print and sing it. It was as if it was a fast-moving train. I wanted to shout, "Wait. Wait for me. I'm your mother and I'm coming with you!" The next year, 1983, I had more invitations to speak and sing in churches in North Carolina, South Carolina, and Georgia. The following year my trips went further afield when I went to West Virginia, Florida, and Tennessee.

"Weave" even found its way to the Girl Scouts of America. One day I got a call from their home office asking if they could use my song for their National and International Conferences. This request was special for me because I'd been a Girl Scout. I was ready to say "Yes" when they said that there was a small problem with my lyrics. It was the fact that the lyrics said, "The Christ in me meets the Christ in thee." The thought of changing the lyrics raised the hairs on the back of my neck. That was the heart of the song that was based on a Quaker saying. They continued, "We are not a Christian organization but are inclusive and welcome all religions, Jewish, Muslim, etc." They asked if they could say, "The Scout in me greets the Scout in thee?"

"It is much bigger than Scout," I said.

"We mean *Big Scout!*"

"It is even bigger than Big Scout."

I said that I needed time to think and pray about it. I called them back the next week and said I would be happy with "The Spirit in me greets the Spirit in thee." They agreed, and that is how it is printed in all the Girl Scout songbooks, including the small yellow paperback songbook that is just like the one I had when I was a Girl Scout!

I began getting calls from Girl Scout chapters in states all over the country requesting permission to reprint "Weave," and for several years I gave permission freely. I wrote many, many letters on the typewriter granting permission, before the days of simple email replies on the computer. I am more of a slap-dash-get-it-done person than a detail one, so that was a tedious chore. I had to use messy carbon paper for my copies and Wite-Out to correct mistakes.

When Sam, our son who has always had a head for business, found out that I was giving copyright permission for free, he argued, "Mom, you need to charge them. You have a unique product and people want it."

I was conflicted: my music had come to me freely as a gift. My dad had instilled that thought in my head at an early age when he said "Your voice is a gift from God. You should never charge a fee." Now as an adult, I wondered if it would be all right for me to charge?

I finally decided to charge a small copyright fee of $10 for a one-time use, and $25 for occasional usage. These fees enabled me to open a music savings account dedicated to future endeavors.

"Weave" continued on its journey even as I suffered the heartache of losing my two major cheerleaders. Jim died suddenly, and Grahame moved back to Australia. However, Grahame's move did take "Weave" down-under, where it was sung in Adelaide by two thousand people who gathered in a stadium to hear the Archbishop of Canterbury. Meanwhile, someone walking down the street humming "Weave," must have carried it from the National Girl Scout office in Philadelphia to the National Lutheran Women's office, because the Lutherans invited me to sing at their National Synod Women's President's meeting in Greenville, South Carolina. After I sang, I sold my cassettes and songbooks. I was overwhelmed when some of the women wanted me to do something I had never done before…autograph my homemade songbooks.

That event opened the door for invitations from other Lutheran churches. One trip took me to sing for a Lutheran Women's Synod in New Jersey, right across the Hudson River from New York City. Leslie went with me, and we were able to go to the theater and do some sightseeing. That fall I got a call from a man who was running for Governor of North Carolina who had heard "Weave" and asked if I would let him use it for his campaign song. I was flattered but said, "No." I couldn't imagine it being tied to one person's political campaign. However, I did give permission for it to be sung at the Democratic National Convention in Atlanta by a black Gospel choir from Morehouse College. Jerry and I went and were tickled pink to hear it sung with a lively Gospel rhythm and clapping!

Even more fun than singing my songs for others was the joy of listening to other people singing my songs back to me. I remembered Peter Yarrow saying that the secret of a song is not the singer nor the song, but the people's singing it that mattered. It was over-the-top to hear it sung by new people in new places. It reminded me of the first time I had heard one of my songs sung by others. It was at an Advance that Jim led one weekend at the Light Center. I had sung "Be Still" many times because it was his favorite. When I walked into that meeting, about one hundred people started spontaneously singing "Be Still." That "stilled" me and brought tears to my eyes.

My song had a life of its own. It was like seeing my child venture out independently and not needing my help anymore.

As "Weave" hit its stride, invitations began coming from many faraway places. I was a newbie and didn't know anyone with whom to consult about setting fees or travel arrangements. I wished that there was someone to talk with who was doing what I was doing. It was such fun to sing and yet I wanted to be paid.

I thought of what the great Ray Charles had said when he came to Asheville and was interviewed by the "Asheville Citizen Times" before his concert. The reporter asked him what he charged, and he replied, "I don't ask for any money to sing. As a matter of fact, I would be willing to pay people to come and listen. But I do charge for travel, rehearsing, setting up, etc.," That's just how I felt. I would sing for free, but I did want to be paid for all my preparation and travel.

How could I determine what my fees would be? I began by charging $25 or $50 for local gigs, such as Kanuga or one-day trips from home, but what to charge when I started going to faraway places? I had hoped that my invitations would come with a set fee offered, but instead there was always their question, "What do you charge?" I began slowly with $100 or $150, and they accepted so quickly that I wondered if I was charging enough? The amount of money to charge was always a dilemma. However, I was glad to deposit these funds in my music savings account, so that I would have money for future recordings.

I needed to find a way to have a reliable sound system but had no idea what to buy. I had quickly learned that I couldn't rely on the local pianists to accompany me, as they were not always accomplished and there was very little time to rehearse. Many times there was an old out-of-tune piano; sometimes even with a missing key like my first time in the basement of the Episcopal church in High Point. I needed a reliable way to be accompanied when I sang, so I asked my recording engineer to make individual soundtrack cassette tapes of each song for me to use as my accompaniment. But how would I play the cassettes and what equipment would be easy for me to handle?

Once more I turned to Howard, and he said I would need an amplifier, speakers, and tape deck. He went with me to a sound equipment shop where we selected what I would need. I bought a pair of speakers with a strong case that would clamp together for travel, and a tape deck for my cassettes. The amplifier I bought was heavy, so I found an old hard suitcase and outfitted it with foam so that the amp would fit snugly. From then on, I traveled with my own sound equipment whether driving or flying. Now I was ready to travel anywhere with my instrumental arrangements in tow. The old TV western, "Have Gun—Will Travel" came to mind. Now I "Had

Music—Will Travel."

Most of the time, traveling and being away from home wasn't difficult for our family, as Leslie was in her last years of high school. Sam was away in college and had recovered from his surgery, even playing golf again. Jerry was always supportive, and rejoiced with me when I received an invitation to go and sing. I knew it wasn't easy for him to take charge when I was away, as he had a busy law practice with clients and trial work, but he never made me feel guilty about leaving. I always looked forward to returning home and sharing my adventures with him as we settled once more into our life until my next gig.

By that time, "Weave" had been published in the Upper Room *Worshipbook,* the Disciples of Christ *Chalice Hymnal,* and the *Unity Hymnal,* as well as *Cursillo* and *Emmaus* songbooks and many parish songbooks. It was the theme song for the1984 Girl Scout/Girl Guide World Conference in New York City, as well as for the Lutheran Women's Convocation when the three branches of the Lutheran Church merged into the Evangelical Lutheran Church of America.

Because of its popularity and because another artist friend, Mimi had designed lovely calligraphy of the words "weave us together in unity and love," I had an idea. I thought of the tee shirts that kids bought when they went to concerts and wondered if I printed Mimi's calligraphy on tee shirts, would people in my audiences buy them? I found a small shop in Weaverville that would print the shirts in bright colors. They were a big success, and soon I had orders from all over the country, and I took them with me when I sang to sell, alongside my records and cassettes. What fun it was to sing someplace and see some of the women wearing "Weave" shirts.

I put up a large map of the United States in my office and stuck blue pins on all the places that had requested permission to sing "Weave," and I put red pins in for where I'd gone in person. It was heart-warming over the next years to see the map filling up with pins. That map was a tangible sign that I had made the right decision to follow my music.

The She of God

I know a lot about the He of God.
Not much about the She of God.
I know a lot about the Father, but Who is my
Mother?
Where is the Other?
Who is my Mother?

The black walnut tree outside my window was still vibrating, and the songs kept on coming. The success of "Weave" made me bolder to speak my own truth, and I was beginning to question all the male images of God and the patriarchy of the church. At that time, the Episcopal church was beginning to ordain women, despite bitter controversy. I was embarrassed to realize that my earlier songs used the male language of "he" and "him" to include everyone. A friend got my attention when she said, "Inclusive language is a justice issue." That was my epiphany. I realized that I and many other women did not feel included in the words men and brothers, and also all of my pronouns for God were masculine.

From then on, I began using inclusive language in my songs. One of my new songs was "The She of God." I read in the book *Children's Letters to God* that a little girl wrote, "Dear God. Are boys better than girls? I know you are one, but try to be fair. Love, Sylvia." I saw a bumper sticker that said, "God is coming soon and is she pissed!"

I went to a workshop led by Brian Wren, a prolific contemporary English hymn writer who was one of the first new hymnodist to write hymns in inclusive language. I was blown away by his hymn, "Bring Many Names," which broke through our stereotypical images of God. Verses included phrases like, "Strong, mother God, working night and day, planning all the wonders of creation," and, "Warm, father God, hugging every child, feeling all the strains of human living." Another was "Old, aching God" and another "Young, growing God." I adored his hymn and knew it would be an integral part of my future programs. It was intriguing to share it with women from all over the country and to hear and see their reactions as they sang this hymn.

In 1989, we recorded a fifth album "In the Beginning Was the Song," and whereas before I had asked male clergy to write on my album covers, this time it was important to me to ask women clergy. So I asked a female Episcopal priest and a female Lutheran pastor to write on the album. I also wrote on the cover,

"My earliest memories are the sounds of THE SONG singing inside of me. As a young child, I responded to it by singing my own songs. I sang for hours alone in a tall cane rocker, singing and singing.

As I grew older I began to hear THE SONG in the world.

I heard it in people and I heard it in creation.

I heard it in joy and wonder, in pain and emptiness.

And I learned that each of us sings our own song.

For THE SONG must be remembered."

One day, I got a call from a woman in South Carolina who was the National President of the Episcopal Church Women. She invited me to present a workshop at the Triennial Convention of Episcopal Church Women in Detroit. I was over the moon! This was my first invitation to perform at an Episcopal national event, and it would be an opportunity to share my music with Episcopal women from all over the country. And hopefully, it might lead to more invitations. I titled my workshop, "Sing to the Lord a New Song." Even though my workshop was only for one morning, I decided to stay for the week and set up a booth with my record albums, cassettes, songbooks, tee shirts, and sweatshirts. I asked my can-do-anything artist friend, Mimi, to figure out how I could create a display. She came up with a large tri-fold board on which I could post my photo and information about me and my music. She also made a tablecloth and a banner for my display. I bought an architect's valise into which I could fit all these items. Now I was ready to travel. I shipped my albums and shirts ahead, and had a wonderful week meeting many new people, attending glorious worship services and hearing inspirational speakers, plus the extra bonus of making many sales. This time over 200 albums, songbooks, and shirts were sold.

At the convention, I sought out the Rector-Elect of a church in Charlotte because I had been invited to come to his church that fall to celebrate his new ministry. I found him in a small office where he was reporting on the convention. He was friendly and glad to meet me ahead of time before the celebration at his new church. Besides his convention reporting, he was also writing the new issue of "Forward, Day by Day," which is the daily devotional published by the Episcopal Church. Later that month, when I read my copy of

"Forward," I was surprised and delighted to read that he had written one week's devotions about my music and dedicated it to me. He wrote, "I remember our first meeting in Detroit, Rosemary. You sought me out in some far corner of Cobo Hall. You greeted me with a smile and open arms...to a new life that I had hardly begun."

I met women who were leaders in their parishes from all over the country, and from then on, I received invitations from California and Oregon, to Minnesota and Iowa. One day a call came from the rector of St. John's Episcopal Church in Charlotte, inviting me to lead his parish weekend retreat at Kanuga. Up until then I had been invited to sing and sometimes give a workshop that lasted one or two hours. When I sang, I usually told the stories of the songs and what had inspired them, so my concerts involved speaking and singing. Now I was being asked to lead a retreat that would cover an entire weekend...about eight or nine hours. YIKES! How could I provide that much content? How would I keep people interested for three days? I'd been to retreats before and remembered how they were structured. There would usually be a Friday night program, then Saturday morning and Saturday afternoon sessions, with sometimes a Saturday night concert or program. On Sunday, a sermon and songs for the worship service. There was also the dilemma of what to charge.

I began to try to figure out how to plan a whole weekend and set aside an entire day to work on the retreat. My special place was in our bedroom in a large blue chair with ottoman beside the window, where I could watch the birds at our bird feeder. That was where I meditated, journaled, and read. As I sat and pondered, I remembered my graduate counseling courses that had taught me how to work with small groups. I looked back on my school teaching days when I'd learned to create lesson plans that would have variety and interest. I thought about my training in Guided Imagery and Music which would help me incorporate quiet listening times. My plans began to evolve as I thought about movement with body prayer, small group exercises and discussions, quiet times to meditate and journal, and of course lots of songs.

I gathered my journals, books, poetry, and the varied notes and quotations that I had collected over the years and placed them all around me...on the ottoman, the large round end table, the floor, and on my lap. Then I sat and wondered what the theme would be. It came immediately: the Quaker saying, "The Christ in me greets the Christ in thee," which is the heart of my song "Weave." Then another saying came to mind, "Whenever a human being approaches, she/he is surrounded by a legion of angels saying, 'Make way for the image of God.'"

I remembered a body prayer that would incorporate movement, and I thought of a simple chant that I'd learned that could be quietly and repeatedly sung in prayer. I thought of all my songs that were on cassettes, and decided which ones would be relevant. I liked to incorporate not only my songs but other music, some popular and some classical, as well as hymns that I would ask our church organist to record on cassettes. I had fifty individual cassettes of the instrumental arrangements of my songs, plus the cassettes that I had made of other music that I could arrange in any order. I could vary my solo singing with group singing and listening.

I thought of personal stories I could share, like my time in the hospital with Sam, or the time when I was directing the choir and had suddenly imagined the face of Jesus imposed on my most difficult choir soprano. (She was the one who sang sour notes.) I remembered other vignettes that would also illustrate my theme. I thought of a group activity for weaving when I remembered how we had woven potholders when we were children. Maybe we could each think of people who had been important in our lives—friends, teachers, mentors, or family—and choose a different color for each of them. Then we could weave the colored strips of paper into a paper potholder, and share the stories of our people in small groups.

This creative period of sorting and gathering ideas was like seeing pieces of a colorful quilt floating all around me. Finally came the fun part of figuring out where each piece would fit. Some pieces fit perfectly, while others were stowed away for future quilts.

Lastly, I had to pay attention to the details…the nitty-gritty of how to structure the retreat. How much time to allow for my speaking segments, and when to intersperse my singing and group singing? I would need to time my talks and songs. How much discussion time for group sharing and group activities? How much quiet time for reflections and prayers? Then there were the handouts. Each person would need song sheets plus the themes with quotes and poetry. I would have to type a master copy and send it ahead. I would also ask the leader to have the construction paper cut and ready.

Gracious! There was a lot to think about and plan and I hoped that I had covered all the bases. After my extensive preparation, I was as ready as I ever would be and headed for my first retreat leading a parish weekend at Kanuga for members of St. John's Episcopal Church from Charlotte. There were about one hundred men and women, and they were enthusiastic and eager to participate. They especially enjoyed the paper-weaving exercise. I received lots of favorable feedback from the people and from their priest.

After that, I was invited to Chesapeake, Virginia, to St. Thomas Episcopal Church to lead a retreat for seventy-five people, and again, I was well received. Being able to sing my music and to share my ideas about God was a rich experience. It was an anxious but also an exciting time for me as I waited for the phone to ring and wondered where my next invitation would take me. I felt like a teenager, waiting and hoping a cute boy would be calling me for a date!

Besides the Episcopal women, Lutheran women called with invitations to Montana, Wisconsin, and Illinois. My calendar was filling up as much as a year in advance. At the retreats I was usually invited to preach on Sunday mornings, so I asked Bishop Weinhauer for a Lay Preaching license, which he graciously gave me. And lo and behold, one Sunday I was even invited to preach in my own Trinity Parish about my impressions of the Triennial. I must have been well received, because later they asked me to preach again, that time with no assigned topic. What a turnaround from my music's first tentative beginning in my home parish, to now being affirmed by my rector and by my parish!

Traveling to unknown places with unknown people was always a little intimidating, as I never knew who would meet me and rarely knew where I would be staying. I usually flew to these retreats, and as I exited the plane and got to the terminal, it was reassuring to see a smiling face holding up a sign that said, "Rosemary Crow." When the retreat was in a hotel or conference center, I was most comfortable staying in a room by myself. That gave me time before and during breaks to have quiet time in order to center myself and also to rest my voice. Before the morning session, I always ordered room service for breakfast to further enjoy my solitude. Retreats usually ended in the late afternoon, so I would spend that night in my room, order room service and enjoy unwinding with a good book and solitaire.

There were some glitches with flying, though, like the time my arrival into Boston had been delayed by several hours. I was planning to check into the hotel and then have time to set up my sound system, but when my plane was delayed, I missed my connection, so I didn't arrive until early evening. By then the participants were already seated for dinner, eating and waiting for the event—which was me! I hastily set my suitcase down, set up my sound system, and began singing. When my presentation was over, I was exhausted but amazed that it went so smoothly. In a flash I had gone from a being frazzled traveler to an energetic presenter. I knew that it had been a job well done.

Sometimes I was scheduled to stay in a home with one of the participants. Many times I met delightful people, but it was tiring to be smiling and talking all the time. The most difficult home-stay was the time when I stayed with a family on a farm in Iowa. They obviously were not accustomed to guests, nor to making hospitable conversation. After my several futile attempts to get a conversation going, we had a silent dinner. The silence was awkward for me and afterwards I excused myself and went to my room.

The circumstances were always different, like the time I was met at the Minneapolis airport by some Lutheran women who were eager to take me to the world's largest indoor mall. They were shocked when I said I just wanted to go to the hotel. Another time I went to a Lutheran camp in Michigan where I had a private room, but it was a camp so the bathroom was a long way down the hall, which made my usual midnight visit to the bathroom challenging. Once there was a day's ECW event that was scheduled in a remodeled old movie theater. My hostess was excited about the venue, but it was awkward for me to be up on the stage looking down at my audience and made me feel like a performer rather than a sharer of songs and stories.

I was invited to lead a retreat at the church where I was raised, Coral Gables First Methodist...this made me incredibly happy. I flew to Miami and was met at the airport by my childhood friend, Sallie. She had a map and directions, since she had never been to the retreat center that the church had rented. It was a long way and in unfamiliar territory. We finally saw the sign, turned off onto a gravel road, and rode through the woods until we came to a locked gate. Soon a heavily-bearded man with his dog appeared and opened the gate He welcomed us and said, "This is my dog, who was possessed by the devil, but I had him exorcised, and he is all right now."

Sallie and I exchanged worried glances as she parked her car. We were both getting bad vibes from him and his weird greeting as we followed him and his dog while he showed us around the camp. There were several small cabins and one larger one where our meeting and meals would take place. Then he led us to a small cabin and said, "This is where you can stay and be by yourself." I usually wanted to stay alone but this man and his camp were so creepy, I said, "Thank you, but Sallie will be staying with me." In spite of our strange beginning, once the retreat started and the women arrived, everything went well.

Another time I flew to Orlando and when I checked in at the hotel, there had been a mix-up and there was no room reserved for me. The manager improvised by setting up a sofa-bed in a cavernous meeting room which was uninviting and anything but conducive to a good night's sleep. My accommodations were never routine and sometimes full of unwelcome surprises. I had to learn to go with the flow.

"Weave" led me to some unexpected places too, like the times I was invited to sing in two different prisons. The first was the local minimum-security prison for women at Black Mountain. Peg, the chaplain asked me to come and sing for the women at their Labor Day picnic. I arrived with my tiny orchestra in my boom box and was greeted by a few young women, most of whom were the ages of my children. They were excited to see the boom box and asked if I had some songs that they knew. I said, "No, I'm a songwriter and this is my own music. You've probably never heard it before." I could see the disappointment on their faces. They were hoping for country or rock songs. About fifteen women settled down on the concrete benches beside the picnic tables and I began to speak and sing. Their faces were passive and their disappointment was palpable. I assumed that because they were in prison, they made no effort to be appreciative and polite. One-by-one they began to drift away and go back to their quarters. Finally, there was no one left but Peg and me. I smiled at Peg and said, "I guess my program is over."

The other prison was a mens' maximum security jail in Columbia, SC. There was an active group of laymen who volunteered there and had asked me to come and sing. It was a sobering experience to enter that large concrete building and go through a series of doors that opened and closed with loud clangs. I was grateful to be well received by about seventy-five male prisoners, most of whom were

African-American. When I finished singing, they were smiling as they told me that they had a surprise for me. Twelve of them formed a chorus kick-line and began to sing and kick as they sang "Weave." The funniest part to me was the way these burly men added some words to the chorus and sang "Weave tra-la-la, Weave tra-la-la." Even though their singing was humorous, it was a moving experience for me to hear the words and music of my song sung back to me in such a venue by such a chorus!

I was beginning to realize that "Weave" no longer belonged to me. It had become a song for anyone to play and sing with his or her own interpretation. This became evident to me when a visiting priest and his wife came to our church and we sang "Weave." His wife told him that I had written it and he said, "Oh no. That song has been around a long time. We sang it in our old church." What a fine compliment that was!

The Song

Long before the World,
First there was the Song.
Long before all Time,
Love Brought forth the Song.
And the song must be remembered.

In the midst of all these trips and engagements, I was still composing, and eager to record yet another album. I hoped Howard would be available as he was now busy with his active and growing church Jubilee! in downtown Asheville. He had left the Methodist Church and had begun a new church based on Matthew Fox's "Creation Spirituality." I called him and asked if he would do another album with me. He said, "Yes, I will help you, if you will take over the main responsibilities." No longer a newbie, I had definite ideas about the instrumental arrangements, and volunteered to chart the songs for the instrumentalists and write the cello arrangements. Eli, our bassist, agreed to write the string arrangements. In the recording studio I was now the one in charge. This time it was a true partnership between Howard and me which felt good and right.

I had written a song for the Rev. Susan Sherard's new Episcopal church in Mars Hill, as well as a tribute to Jim, "Farewell, Old

Friend." My song, "Sara Laughed," made me think of my good friend, Anne who had the most contagious, infectious laugh, just like Sara's. The chorus said,

> *Sara laughed. Oh how she laughed.*
> *It started with a giggle that went right up thru her middle,*
> *To a chuckle bursting forth, then a chortle, then a roar.*
> *She threw back her head and she laughed.*

I asked Anne to come to the studio so that we might record her laughing. She was hesitant, but reluctantly agreed. When she arrived, she seemed intimidated by the studio and musicians, and I wondered if we would be able to get her laughing. Finally, she loosened up as we rehearsed; she heard Howard laughing as Jesus in the second verse, and then all of us laughing as the wild group of people on the first Pentecost. By that time, we were all laughing and Anne, with her uproarious laugh cut loose and laughed as Sara in the first verse. I always enjoyed performing that song because her laugh was so infectious that the audience could not help but join me in laughing.

When we recorded our sixth album "Where There is Love" in 1989, we did not order any records. Young people may not have ever seen a record, (a large black disk that has to be played by a needle on a turntable) although I understand that they are now making a comeback as retro. Records were bulky and easily scratched and were fast becoming obsolete. This time we only ordered cassettes. Since the finished product was no longer a large record album cover but the size of a cassette, I only had room on the cover for a photo of me at the piano, and there was no room for album notes. When the new cassettes arrived, we gave another concert at Trinity. Again, it was wonderful to sing with live musicians rather than my tiny orchestra in a box! Little did I know that this would be my last concert at Trinity.

We had a new rector and there was trouble brewing at Trinity. I had been on the Search Committee when we had called him and that had been a difficult decision. Our top two choices had turned us down, and we had grave doubts when we called our third choice, but he came and it was a disaster for us. He was depressed and distant. Many left the church and attendance and giving dwindled Sunday by Sunday. Trinity was split between those who wanted him to stay, and those who thought he should leave. It began to create a divide that seemed to be mostly between the younger women and the older men. There was a small group of us who were labeled the "Seven Savage Women," which was hurtful. It seemed that my long history with the church as Director of Music didn't matter one whit, and some of those people who had always supported me, turned against me. It was a painful time for all of us.

One unmistakable sign for me that the joy had gone out of Trinity was when Jimmy left. Jimmy was a mentally challenged young man who had worshipped with us for many years. Every Sunday he'd brought his gifts of art, which were small stained glass pieces encased with metal strings that could be hung in a window to reflect the light. He was always smiling as he offered them as gifts to us. One day we noticed that he was no longer coming and we learned that he had gone up the street to the Methodist church. He truly was our canary in the coal mine and when he left, we knew that the joy was gone from Trinity. About that same time mercifully our Rector resigned, and the church began looking for an interim Rector.

Meanwhile, I was becoming more and more comfortable and brave about speaking from my own inner authority. I had moved from being a Pleaser/Performer to a Proclaimer. When I led a retreat in Little Rock, Arkansas, I spoke strongly about the need for inclusive language and for feminine images of God, even though their Bishop was there listening. I could see him standing in the back, but this bishop was not scowling. Rather he was intently listening. I was wondering what he was thinking about my lyrics and was thankful when later he told me that my words had opened up new images and ideas for him. I found it a privilege to go to new places because many times when I met strangers, they would skip the small talk and immediately begin the conversation on a deep level. They were honest and vulnerable as they shared their personal stories.

During that time, I was serving on the Program Committee at Kanuga and our job was to plan the conferences and decide whom we would invite to be the main presenters. I thought that Kanuga should host a Christian Feminist Conference and I volunteered to coordinate it. Since the ordination of women priests had recently happened, it seemed a timely topic. I envisioned that this would be a popular summer conference with about two hundred participants, so I was disappointed and surprised when only eighty women signed up.

I invited the Rev Carter Heyward, one of the "Philadelphia Eleven" who were the first women to be ordained, and Bishop Barbara Harris, who was the first woman to be consecrated Bishop in the Episcopal Church. I also invited Dr Delores Williams, a womanist theologian and author of the book *Sisters in the Wilderness,* and a gifted African-American poet, Glennis Redmond. This was a stellar cast of presenters whose talks were brilliant and moving as they challenged the structure of the male hierarchy in the church and taught us some of the many overlooked stories of women in the Bible. Since we were a small group, our meeting place was in the room beneath the dining room. It was an uninviting space with low ceilings, so once again I called on Mimi, my artist friend, to brighten up the room, which she did with colorful streamers and posters. The participants were a congenial group who were eager to hear from our outstanding presenters. There was much laughter, sharing, and a good camaraderie as we enjoyed our time together.

However, we could not help but notice one young woman who always sat alone in the back typing on her laptop. We soon found out that she had been sent to report about our conference by a conservative Episcopal magazine. We called her "the spy." On the last day, I spontaneously sang my song, "You Can Be a Heretic, Too!" I had never performed it before in public, but this seemed the right time and place. The following month I was proud to see that my song was quoted in that publication not as noteworthy, but rather as unworthy!

One day, a woman called and invited me to present a workshop at the national ECW Triennial in Phoenix. Just as the Triennial in Detroit three years ago, this would again be an opportunity to meet women from all over the country. I was beginning to think about the thousands and thousands of images of God, so I decided to call my workshop, "O For a Thousand Tongues to Sing." I engaged our church organist to record several hymns on cassette tapes including the hymn "O For a Thousand Tongues to Sing" for the opening song. My workshop description said,

God sings and speaks to us in many voices - sometimes familiar, and sometime surprising; sometimes ordinary and sometimes mysterious; sometimes still and small and sometimes earthshaking. Even if we had a thousand tongues, we could not respond to all of these voices. But we can explore and share how we hear and answer them through songs, poetry, stories, movement and silence.

I was given a room in the hotel by the convention for the week with the caveat that I might have a different roommate from time to time. Late one night after I had been asleep, I realized that a new roommate had entered the room. In a few hours I heard the shower running; I looked at my clock and saw that it was four AM. I was afraid that she hadn't set her clock to Central Time, so I knocked on the bathroom door to tell her (I hoped it was a Her!) what time it was. A female voice answered, and she said that she knew the time and she continued with her shower. I went back to sleep and when I woke the next morning, she was gone. I never found out who she was. Happily, there were no other roommates.

That workshop morphed into plans for a new retreat called "Images of God." Once again, I enjoyed creating my quilt as I gathered the pieces that would encourage the participants to explore as many images of God as they could name and imagine. I took a kaleidoscope and used it for a hands-on experience for each one to hold and see how the images varied with just a flick of the wrist, which was how quickly our images changed from person to person. Besides my own songs, I recorded other music such as "The 23rd Psalm" by Bobby McFerrin, "I Don't Know How to Love Him" from "Jesus Christ, Superstar," and "Alleluia" from Honnegar's "King David." I accompanied my presentation with art prints to pass around, such as the masculine God by Michelangelo in the Sistine Chapel, The Laughing Christ, and a colorful painting of the cosmos by an artist friend that I had used as the album cover of "In The Beginning was the Song."

I opened with a funny story about a little boy who told his mother that he knew God's name. She asked him, "What is it?" He said "Andy." His mother was puzzled. She asked, "Why did he think that?" The boy said, "We sing his name in the hymn in church... and he (andy) walks with me, and he (andy) talks with me." That was a good ice breaker for the beginning of the retreat. One exercise I planned was for each participant to draw a timeline of the important events in their lives. Then I asked them to write an image of God by each event and to ponder whether their images were different or had stayed the same. I also had a large white paper posted on the wall on which they could write their images of God as they thought of them during the weekend. At the end of the weekend, I copied those images on little strips of paper and put them in a basket. During the worship service on Sunday, each person drew out one of the strips with an image that I hoped would speak to each one individually. Later I received letters and notes saying that it was a powerful retreat that had made an impact on many of them.

However, there was one strong negative reaction to my retreat, "Images of God." It happened when I took it to Iowa for a retreat of the women of the Reformed Church of America (RCA). I did not know that this was a very conservative church, nor did they realize that I was a wide-open seeker and presenter. As I flew in, I looked out the window of the plane and saw straight roads with no curves. This turned out to be a metaphor for the weekend. They were the straight lines, and I was a curvy road, and never the twain would meet. It was a time when I did the best I could and was met with stony faces. Their faces reminded me of the Episcopal priest's scowling face when I did my first tentative singing of my songs fourteen years ago and was met with a stony reception. My visit with the RCA was the only time I was not well received, and I vowed in the future to do some research on the inviting group before I accepted an invitation.

A few of my trips were particularly memorable, like the one for the women in the Disciples of Christ Church in Oklahoma City. They were a remarkable group: open and inviting. They took me to see the site of the recent terrible Oklahoma bombing that had killed so many people, including children. We saw the make-shift memorial where those grieving had placed flowers, pictures, and even a teddy bear. Seeing the devastation of this tragic event inspired me to write a song for them, "Deep Peace," which I set to the words of a Celtic prayer.

With all my traveling, singing, and speaking, I longed for some retreat time for myself; time to settle down, relax, listen, and be renewed. Whenever I sang near the ocean, I would stay over a few extra days to unwind and once again *enter the silence deep in the heart of God.* Nothing filled my soul more than walking on a lonely beach and listening to the waves and watching the gulls. Once when I was singing in Lexington, Kentucky, I decided to go on a planned retreat. I knew that the Trappist Monastery at Gethsemane where Thomas Merton had lived was not far away, so I had called the center a few weeks ahead and made a reservation for a silent retreat. I knew that I would relish the silence, especially after my gig of non-stop talking for two days.

It was late afternoon when I drove into a lovely green space that seemed an oasis set apart from the world. There was a plain white two-story building with a chapel spire beckoning. I parked my car, got my suitcase and timidly approached the main door. When I walked into the reception area, my first impression was simplicity. The wooden floors were sparkling clean and the few chairs and sofa were neatly arranged. I spotted a monk who was smiling as he walked towards me. He said, "You must be Rosemary. I am Brother John. Let me be the first to welcome you to Gethsemane. Give me your bag and I'll show you to your room." On the way to my room, he pointed out the chapel and the refectory, and then we climbed the stairs and came to my room. He opened the door and I saw an austere room with a small bed, desk, and bathroom. I was beginning to have doubts and wondering why in the world I'd come here when I saw the plaque on the wall which was a quote from Thomas Merton: "A place apart to entertain silence in the heart and listen for the voice of God." My eyes teared up and I knew that I was in the right place.

The monk gave me a schedule for the services and meals, as well as the house rules and said that a bell would ring soon to give five minutes notice for Vespers. He left and just as I got settled, the 5:30 bell rang. I went to the chapel and read the sign that pointed guests to the small balcony where I sat down next to two other guests who were already seated. Then we heard footsteps and watched the robed monks silently enter below us and take their seats on either side of the choir stalls. When they began to chant, the air was filled with an ethereal sound. We guests did not participate but silently let the liturgy envelop us. After Vespers, another bell sounded calling us to dinner and there I had the opportunity to look at the monks who were seated with me around the long refectory table. There were about twenty ordinary looking men of all ages. I didn't spot Brother John because in their robes all the monks looked alike. Other than the sounds of the chairs being pulled out from the table, there was silence, and while we were eating, a monk began to read aloud a meditation.

After dinner, I walked around outside before a 7:30 bell rang summoning us to Compline. After the service, the monastery settled down for the night and all was quiet. It was an early hour for me, so I read for a long while before falling asleep. It seemed just a few minutes before I was awakened at 3:15 by a bell ringing for Vigils. I thought, "This is the middle of the night," and it was! I didn't make it to that service, but did go to Lauds when the 5:45 bell rang. After that another bell for the 6:15 Eucharist, and then on to have a silent breakfast.

During the next day, I took several walks in the woods and read and journaled. I didn't see any of the monks and assumed they were at their chores in the kitchen or on the grounds. I found myself always listening for the bells so that I didn't miss lunch, or the late after-noon call for Vespers. That night after dinner I saw a monk stand-ing outside. I had read in the house rules that talking was permitted after dinner in designated areas and he was standing in that area. I surprised myself by asking him if I could talk with him. He nodded and probably thought that I had some deep questions, but rather I just wanted to hear a human voice talk about ordinary things like the weather. While we were chatting, the bell sounded for Compline. The next morning after Lauds and Eucharist, I ate my silent breakfast while listening to another monk read. After breakfast, I packed my bag and loaded the car. I treasure the time I spent at Gethsemane and will always remember the bells and the rich silence.

Sometimes my trips took me to beautiful places and after my singing, I would spend a couple of days sightseeing. Once I was invited to Buffalo to sing for a meeting of the Episcopal Diocese in Western New York. I knew that Pat Flanagan, whom Leslie had married last summer, was from the town of Geneseo, not too far from Buffalo. After my gig, I rented a car and drove there. I had called his Aunt Susan ahead of time and she had graciously agreed to meet me. That day she showed me Pat's home, his school, and his church, and told me stories about him and his family. Seeing those places and hearing the stories made me feel like I knew him better, which was important to me since he was now a member of our family. Before flying home, I also drove to Niagara Falls. I had been there many years before with Jerry, but wanted to see it again. It was crowded with tourists like me, but the crowds didn't take away from the awesome power of the falls.

A trip to Portland, Oregon, was fun because Jerry went with me. He spent the day golfing while I was leading a retreat. Afterwards we stayed a few days vacationing in that beautiful state.

Once when I was singing for the Lutheran women in South Dakota, I decided to be a tourist once again. Since I was near the Black Hills and the Badlands, I rented a car to drive and see Mount Rushmore and the Crazy Horse Memorial. The huge rock monuments loomed large and were stark against a brilliant blue sky. The rock formations were shades of orange and umber, which was so different from our lush green Blue Ridge Mountains. I'll have to admit that it was not as much fun sightseeing on my own. I would rather be sharing the experience with Jerry, but when I was in new territory I wanted to take advantage of the opportunity. After my traveling it was always good to come home again to Jerry and our home in the woods.

Changes

Changes almost always hurt,
And hurting always changes.
Changes almost always hurt,
And hurting always changes, rearranges,
always changes.

Our family life was undergoing big changes. Jerry's father had died and we were assuming the responsibilities of caring for his mother. After Leslie married Pat, he was commissioned into the army and they moved to Ft. Hood, Texas. Soon they had a baby, our first grandchild! One perk of my travels was that I was able to see them and our grandson, Houghton often, as my travel agent would arrange three-legged air flights. No matter where I traveled, I could arrange to stop off in Texas on my way home. My mother was diagnosed with Alzheimers, and was angry and depressed. Dad was overcome with sadness and was at loose ends. They moved in with my brother and his wife, which didn't work out, and my brother and I were at odds about how to help them. He moved to Oregon and took our parents with him. Mother died there within a few months. It was painful to lose her and to have Dad so far away. A few months later, I flew out to Oregon and brought my dad to Asheville to live in a retirement place near us.

With all these changes going on, I began to think about a new album, "Changes," which I didn't know at the time, but it would be our last album. I had written a wedding song for Leslie, "Here you Now Stand" and a song about the trouble in our church, "Walk Through the Rain." I had also written a song "Saturday Phone Call" about my mother's Alzheimer's. That was the one song that I never could perform because I couldn't sing it without crying.

Once again, Howard and I worked on the musical arrangements. This recording would be different because, for the first time we would record digitally, and instead of records or cassettes, we would produce our first Compact Disc (CD). One unexpected bonus was that Howard knew Eugene Frieson who was the cellist with the Paul Winter Consort and invited him to come and play with us. With his beautiful cello playing, he laid down three separate solo tracks for Leslie's wedding song. In the recording studio, I was overjoyed with the clean, clear sound our voices and instruments made. Mary Beth painted a beautiful butterfly to use on the cover to embody changes. When the finished album came out in 1992, we wanted to do another concert at Trinity. I set the date with the musicians and was sure that I had set the date on the church's calendar.

As the date drew near, I checked with our interim rector, who said that there was a conflict on the calendar for that night and we could not use the church. What a blow that was! It brought up all my hurt, because once again my church had rejected me. Did my own parish not want to celebrate my new album? Did no one care? After that bad news, I drove home at dusk in a soft rain which was falling just like my tears. When I stopped at the traffic light, I noticed the car right in front of me with an unusual license plate. I squinted my eyes to read it through the raindrops. To my amazement the license plate read "LUV ROSE." I couldn't believe my eyes, but there it was. It made me smile and know that it would be okay. Later, I talked with Howard and he invited me to give our concert at his church, Jubilee! We did, and it was a grand event. How far we had come and how much the music and I had changed.

I was getting tired of presenting the same theme over and over, so I began to plan a new retreat which I named "Brooding, Birthing, Blessing." I started working on a new music quilt as I gathered songs like Neil Diamond's "Santus" from the movie "Jonathon Livingston Seagull," Bette Midler's "The Wind Beneath my Wings," David Wilcox's "I Feel You Behind Me," and the St Louis Jesuits' "Be Not Afraid." I included poetry by Frederich Buechner, Mary Oliver, Carl Sandburg, Ranier Marie Rilke, and Annie Dillard, and an excerpt from the book, *The Velveteen Rabbit*. The format easily divided into three parts, which fit nicely with the three days' retreat. I thought of brooding as a time of pondering and wondering who God is calling us to be and what She is calling us to do. In Birthing we are finding our own voice, our own power and risking sharing it with others as we are becoming real like the Velveteen Rabbit. Finally, as we move out into the world we are Blessing. After a while, we begin brooding and the whole cycle begins again.

With my new album, "Changes," and my new retreat, "Brooding, Birthing, Blessing," I was invited to lead other events and retreats with Lutherans and Episcopalians. For the next seven years, I traveled to Ohio, Boston, and Chicago and even farther away to San Francisco, Minnesota, Washington State, and Arizona. It was a glorious and fulfilling time for me. One day, I was invited to lead a retreat for a small group of twenty Episcopal women in Chesapeake Virginia in 1999. While I was there, a strange thing happened. All of a sudden, it was as if I were standing outside of myself and realizing that I was tired of listening to myself saying and singing the same things. The spark had gone out, and there was little enthusiasm. I knew in that instant that my journey was coming to an end. I didn't want to lead retreats anymore. The passion had disappeared. I was tired of traveling and wanted to stay home.

Once more, my inner knowing was absolute. It was that same inner knowing that led me to resign my job at Trinity and also to leave Jim and the Light Center. Now it was telling me that It was time to stop before I got stale and hackneyed. Just as suddenly as my music journey began, now suddenly I knew that it was over.

Epilogue

Now, twenty-plus years later, I'm looking back with a grateful heart. I had been led on a journey from being Director of Music at Trinity Church to being catapulted into the new and sometimes scary adventures of composing, and beginning to sing in public again. Somehow, I was given the courage to embark on an uncharted course of speaking and singing all over the country.

I came to understand that the woman's voice that I had first heard singing to me in a dream, was in fact my own voice coming from the Spirit deep within. It was opening my ears and heart to hear new songs. As I was given this gift of songs, I struggled to find my own authority; to have the courage to speak and sing the words just as they had come to me. My images of God were expanding and changing as I embraced the feminine in Mother God. I began to hear Her voice speaking to me as I listened to other people. I recaptured my childhood imagination when I saw Creator God in the fierce energy of the ocean, as well as in the smallest starfish. As I learned to become still, She was there waiting for me, and I began to have a deeper awareness of the "God in whom we live and move and have our being."

The lyrics of my songs were teaching me and affirming how much God loves us and longs for us to know that we are created in His/Her image. Some songs offered thanks for the myriad wonders of creation, and some were about loneliness, betrayal, and loss. Many of the songs began with a "lump in my throat" as the poet Robert Frost said about his poetry. Sometimes the lyrics were controversial and were challenged by church authority figures, but the words came from deep within me and I could not and would not change them. I remembered my covenant with God, which gave me the courage to sing and speak the truth as I understood it. I knew that I had been given a marvelous gift and that I was called to share it with others. The more songs I shared, the more songs I was given. I came to believe what the author, Fred Buechner had written, that my "vocation was when my great joy met the world's great hunger." I received many letters from people whom I'd met in different places and they shared their stories with me. They affirmed my knowing that I was on the right path.

Looking back, I realize that when I heard my first song, "Holy Silence," I took my first tentative step into the unknown, ready to listen and to follow the Holy Spirit as She was calling me. This journey has been easier because of the talented people who were right there when I needed them. First there was Howard, who guided my every step in arranging the music and recording. The joy of performing live with him and his group took me over the moon! Then my dear friend, Mary Beth who was more than a sister as we shared our spiritual journeys in our small prayer group and later in Jim Goure's group. She was always, after Jerry, my first listener of new songs, and a gifted artist who designed my album covers and my flyers. Then, there was Mimi, my can-do-anything friend who created my "traveling show" with the tri-fold board, posters and tablecloth, designed my Weave shirts and also brightened up the basement room for the Feminist Conference at Kanuga. What a gift God gave me in these three friends who nurtured and prepared the way for me to *sing*! Most importantly, there was always Jerry, the "wind beneath my wings," who encouraged me and beamed with pride as I went away to sing while he held down the fort at home.

During all that time, I was in a deep relationship with the Holy Spirit and my prayer life was a passionate love affair. Now years later, as a grandmother in my eighties, I'm looking back on my relationship with Her, which is no longer as intense, but rather the quiet, comfortable one of a long-standing relationship. I am no longer singing and speaking, but rather just being and enjoying our family which has expanded; Sam married Sharon and had two children, Bennett and Rosemary, and Leslie and Pat had three children, Houghton, Laney, and Eliza: our five amazing grandchildren. I no longer hear new songs, and we have moved away from our house in the woods where the black walnut tree vibrated musical notes to me. I left my home church for awhile when I felt that it had rejected me, but after many years I returned and received a warm welcome. Now, once again I enjoy the music, the liturgy and the people. I am pleased that the Episcopal Church has many women priests and bishops, and that the revised *Book Of Common Prayer* and *Hymnal* has language that is more inclusive. Now whenever our congregation recites the "Nicene Creed," I insert feminine pronouns for the Holy Spirit and I say, "With the Father and the Son, SHE is worshiped and glorified. SHE has spoken through the prophets."

I have retained the copyright of "Weave" so that I can have the joy of knowing when and where it is being sung. It has been published in the hymnals of the United Church of Christ, Unity, and the Church of Latter Day Saints, as well as the Upper Room Worshipbook, and my favorite still being the little yellow Girl Scout songbook.

There is nothing more to say except "Thanks be to God."

Albums and Songbooks by Rosemary Crow

1976 "Be Still" - LP, Cassette and Songbook
1977 "In the Stillness" - LP, Cassette & Songbook
1979 "Holy Silence" - LP, Cassette & Songbook
1982 "Go in Peace" - LP, Cassette & Songbook
1986 "In the Beginning Was the Song" - LP, Cassette & Songbook
1989 "Where There is Love" - Cassette & Songbook
1992 "Changes" - CD & Songbook

For permission to use "Weave" and to order Songbooks and recordings, Rosemary my be contacted at 69singer7gmail.com or her website rosemarycrowweave.com

Rosemary and Jerry.

Children and grandchildren.

Made in the USA
Columbia, SC
22 September 2021